BUSINESS BIBLE
FOR SURVIVAL

HOW TO ORDER:

Quantity discounts are available from the publisher, Prima Publishing & Communications, P.O. Box 1260ADS, Rocklin, CA 95677; telephone (916) 624-5718. On your letterhead include information concerning the intended use of the books and the number of books you wish to purchase.

U.S. Bookstores and Libraries: Please submit all orders to St. Martin's Press, 175 Fifth Avenue, New York, NY 10010; telephone (212) 674-5151.

BUSINESS BIBLE
FOR SURVIVAL

What to Do When Your
Company Falls on Hard Times

A. David Silver

Prima Publishing and Communications
P.O. Box 1260ADS
Rocklin, CA 95677
(916) 624-5718

Typography by R. Nolan & Sons
Production by Bookman Productions

Prima Publishing & Communications
Rocklin, CA

Library of Congress Cataloging-in-Publication Data

Silver, A. David (Aaron David), 1941–
   [When the bottom drops]
   Business bible for survival: what to do when your company falls on hard times/ A. David Silver
     p. cm.
   Previously published as: When the bottom drops. 1988.
   ISBN 1-55958-009-7
1. Corporate turnarounds—Management. 2. Business enterprises—Finance. 3. Corporations—Finance. I. Title.
   HD58.8.S57   1990
   658.4' 063—dc20   89-10792
                                           CIP

89   90   91   RRD   10   9   8   7   6   5   4   3   2   1

Printed in the United States of America

DEDICATION

To
Steven H. Caller
Arnold G. Cohen
S. David Morrison

CONTENTS

ACKNOWLEDGMENT

This book is the result of many years' experience in seemingly disastrous business circumstances. Business can be rough. I have been bucked and trampled by bankruptcy, isolation, and shuttered loan windows—like a bad day at the rodeo. I have been knocked down, stomped on, and generally ground in the dust from one side of the ring to the other. But as any seasoned wrangler will tell you, you win when you get up one time more than you get knocked down. I have been involved in more than two hundred work-outs, turn-arounds, and start-ups, and as the dust clears, there I am, standing, ready, and waiting to take my next ride. But you can't keep this up unless you know what you're doing.

"Are there rules for survival in hard times?" That's what my publishing agent, Jeff Herman, asked when we were at the Oyster Bar in Grand Central recently.

I thought a minute and said, "There may be. Let me see if I can come up with them."

"Well, if you do, now more than ever, there is a book that needs to be written," said Jeff, always on the prowl for a good story.

That is how *Business Bible for Survival* got started. It turned out that the survival game is systematic, rather than reflexive, and dragging that system out of me required the pulling, kneading, strong editing, and cajoling of both Jeff Herman and my publisher, Ben Dominitz.

I have known the substance of the survival business for some time, but Jeff and Ben produced the form. Therefore, I gratefully acknowledge their devoted efforts.

A. David Silver
Santa Fe, New Mexico
November, 1989

PREFACE

One of America's favorite sons, Walt Whitman, urged us to "make much of the negatives." This book echoes his charge then shows you how to do it.

Fortunes are made in hard times and lost in good times. Engaging in feckless behavior, failing to acknowledge accountability, growing a business too fast and too soon—these are some of the bad habits we fall into when the economy is good, growing steadily in what we perceive to be a certain, predictable path. When we are lured in a new direction by vanity and curiosity—those sexy twins—our skills cannot carry us. But when we stick to our skills—to what we do best—we perform well. If we anticipate hard times and prepare ourselves with responses to adversity, the resources we need in order to ride out the crisis will be there. Yet, to survive a difficult period, we need more than skills. We need the capital, the time, the fearlessness, and a plan.

Did you know that practically every successful business has sprung from a plan that was created in response to uncertain or difficult times? Today, uncertainty is all around us. The federal government is jaw-boning, insisting that our economy is strong. With its wild swings, the stock market is telling us that there are at least as many pessimists as there are optimists. The new issue window appears closed, then open, then closed. The dollar falls against foreign currencies, then gains momentum, then falls some more. No one understands where the economy is going—no one! A doomsayer fears being caught taking a risk, but he doesn't tell you that he's just put all his assets into gold coins. You cannot trust anyone; they are bluffing just as you are.

A Chart for Turbulent Times

I have been hanging paper in a wind tunnel ever since I launched my investment banking firm in 1970. My specialty has been troubled companies, and I have been assisting businesspeople with buy-outs, work-outs, and start-ups ever since. Nothing in business frightens me, no matter how adverse. And no matter how negative or impossibly hopeless a situation appears, I have learned how to turn adversity into success.

Let me assure you that no matter how frightened you may be about the seriousness of your business problems, you are not alone. I have been through hundreds of business crises, as many people have. We have blazed trails and left markers to guide others through the wilderness of crisis, and I have recorded the markers on a chart for you. That chart is spread out before you, in the form of this book.

You might regard the survival of your business as a game and yourself as the principal player. Relate your business to any team sport you enjoy, and think of yourself as the captain of the team. You have recently learned that a crisis has stricken your team just two weeks before a major tournament, and there appears to be no way you can make it through those two weeks, let alone play in the tournament. I will show you how to get to the tournament, how to compete at top form, and how to win the whole enchilada!

The object of the survival game is to maintain your status as a player and to win with such brilliance that your competition, your lenders, your customers, and your suppliers will speak your name in awe and amazement.

There are four stages to the survival game:

Stage One: Forecasting the effects of uncertainty
Stage Two: Creating genuine liquidity
Stage Three: Learning back-to-the-wall street-fight tactics
Stage Four: Creating and executing a redirect-and-grow plan

A crisis has settled on your company, giving you the opportunity to show your marketplace just how great you really are. To survive, you need to forecast the depths of the crisis, create cash, buy time, adopt backdoor strategies in case the crisis deepens, and then implement a redirect-and-grow plan. This book is divided according to the four stages of survival in order to help you steer your business through the hard times to victory. You may be surprised at the multitude of possibilities and strategies you can employ during a crisis, strategies you might never think of when things are going well. Just bear in mind, there are many people who will suffer if your business fails, so if you treat them with clarity up front and with high ethics throughout your informal reorganization and redirect-and-grow phase, they will cooperate fully with you. These people can be drawn into your nuclear business family to help you "make much of the negatives."

Now, many of you have never experienced hard times; you are like young soldiers not yet battle-scarred. That is why you need to read—no, study—this book. Moreover, you must make certain that your war buddies study this book as well. Your company's survival depends on it.

FORECASTING THE EFFECTS OF UNCERTAINTY

Chapter One

These Are Hard Times

You may not yet feel the need for a chart to help you guide your business through hard times. Things may be going pretty well in your corner of the economic jungle. Your hunters may be bringing in the tigers. Your trappers may be hitting their numbers. Your skinners may be performing at the top of their form. And your traders may be swapping your tiger-skin rugs for the finest beads and spears you have ever set eyes on. Even your hut builders are celebrating by redecorating the walls of your office with scenes of accomplishments, feasts, and new wealth.

But faint drumbeats echoing from a distant mountaintop warn you that something might be wrong. Doubt casts a shadow over you. You grow uncertain. There are events beyond your control. A few hunters mutter about some tigers that got away. Your skinners complain about the low levels of raw material. Your traders come back to the village with second-rate beads. You ask the tribal elders for their opinions, but empty stares greet you. Then your witch doctor says the one word you did not want to hear, "Depression."

WHAT MAKES US NERVOUS

Most of us have not lived through a depression, and only some of us were in management positions during the last serious recession. Reading about the factors that caused business after business to fail is not the same as having been there; crises are so quickly dismissed once they are over. They are much more traumatizing on the way in.

Whether in the economic jungle or in the defense of our national security, crises can catch us sleeping—just as the U.S. Navy was caught off guard while protecting oil tankers in the Persian Gulf in late 1987. Although fully equipped and staffed with a complement of trained seamen, one of the ships was struck because its untested crew did not respond appropriately to the situation. Or consider Itel Corporation. One of the largest and most rapidly growing computer-leasing companies in the 1970s, Itel declared bankruptcy in 1981 because its management refused to recognize the consequences of losing their computer-lease insurance program at the same time that IBM announced cuts and product extensions.* Or consider Finley, Kumble, which grew by acquisition to become one of the country's largest law firms and burst apart because of self-destructive warfare between its principals. Or, finally, consider Donald Burr, founder and chief executive officer of People Express, who wanted to go "big time" with his small airline and acquired a gaggle of other carriers in order to get there fast. Burr finally realized, admittedly too late, that his company was in trouble when his mother told him, "I hope you don't mind but I'm flying American. Just a few dollars more."** People Express, which offered Greyhound-low prices plus convenience, had a focused and defensible idea. But when it expanded too fast—falling victim to those tempting twins, vanity and curiosity—it was not ready, and People Express crashed.

Unpreparedness is caused by the following: (1) rookie-itis, or lacking previous exposure to crises; (2) cognitive dissonance,

---

* *Examiner's Report*, In re Itel Corporation, United States Bankruptcy Court, Northern District of California, March 1981.

** *Inc.* (April 1987), p. 24.

or hearing selective and therefore distorted signals from the marketplace; and (3) bull-headed expansion, or having a management team that's afraid to tell the emperor he's wearing no clothes.

If you are nervous about the onset of tough times, it's because you are not ready. Many of you have never faced really bad times, and the present economy makes you tremble unassured. It should. These are nervous times in business. You and I cocked our ears for history's warnings, but "The venal torrent, murm'ring from afar, whisper'd no peace to calm this nervous war."*

The good times in our economy have run nearly a decade, and many managers suffer from rookie-itis. They hear the "venal torrent" from their sales managers, who complain of foreign imports; from their production foremen, who announce that key suppliers are no longer able to ship; and from their chief financial officers, who report that new cautionary policies are being introduced by the banks. These whispers and murmurs mean something. Should the company retract? Should it entrench? Sell out? Acquire? Should it pay to see the next card, or should it fold? What should one do in unstable times?

READINESS

The best response to uncertain times is to be ready for a crisis. Managers must make their companies mentally and physically prepared for a prompt response to crisis. Personnel from top to bottom must be ready for a quick rebound from setbacks. I am talking about war and about avoiding a Pearl Harbor-type attack: dodging the bullets of an invading competitor, eluding the crosscut of a raider, parrying the sword-thrust of a frightened lender's writ of attachment or escaping the cash starvation of a large customer defaulting on its obligations.

This book is not just for chief executive officers. *This book is intended to prepare for action every person in the company on*

---

* Thomas Harte, as quoted in Samuel Johnson, *A Dictionary of the English Language* (1767).

whom the responsibility for the survival of the company depends. I am not talking about everyday problem solving in this book. I am not talking about the circumvention of the flotsam from work-a-day situations. What I *am* talking about is survival.

SURVIVAL

The story is not a pretty one, but it must be told. Your company's survival is at stake, and you must make sure that all of your potential war buddies read this book, understand its rules, and incorporate them into daily procedures. If you fail to do this, your company may end up like Itel, People Express, or the Finley, Kumble law firm—financially devastated by *avoidable* crises. Itel's management did not listen to the signals from its industry. People Express expanded too fast to fly with the big boys. Finley, Kumble was torn by dissension, conflict, and strife within ranks that were not crisis-trained. These companies were not ready. They did not recognize uncertainty, and they hit the wall in good times. We are not in good times, no matter what some experts say. We are in feverish times. I know we are, because I am a medic on the business battlefield. Every businessperson should be preparing for survival, the survival of his or her business.

This is a tough-talking book. It helps you avoid all-out war and protect your territory by proper planning. And further, if war is unavoidable, this book trains you in battlefield strategies. You are reading the business equivalent of Sun Tzu's *The Art of War,* exhumed and translated in 1963* and considered the "first known attempt to formulate a rational basis for the planning and conduct of military operations."**

Survival depends on recognizing uncertainty for what it is: a crisis about to happen. Uncertainty is a *stressor event.* It creates tensions and pressures much like those that befall a fresh

---

* Sun Tzu, *The Art of War* (circa 500 B.C.). Translated by Samual B. Griffith (Oxford University Press, 1963).
** *The Times* (London, 1963).

recruit facing battle for the first time. Stressor events can cause a loss of balance, a lashing out at stop-gap solutions, and a denial of the horror that, in your heart, you know can result. As a manager, you want to gather your key personnel into your conference room like a trusted commander instilling confidence in his troops. You want to give the stressor event a name. Call it what it is: a pending crisis. Talk about it. Describe its potential effects. Formulate a plan for survival before anything happens.

Here is where this book comes in. It shows you how to step carefully around the mine fields that uncertain times produce, and it gives you a medic's kit with which to survive every imaginable business crisis. As Sun Tzu wrote 2,500 years ago, battles are won without loss of life only by realizing that the primary battlefield is in the mind of the opposing commander. "A skilled general must be master of the complementary arts of simulation and dissimulation; while creating shapes to confuse and delude the enemy, he conceals his true dispositions and ultimate intent. When capable, he feigns incapacity; when near, he makes it appear that he is far away; when far away, that he is near."*

If you are a manager who has never been tested on the battlefield with your company's existence at stake, you are not sufficiently battle-scarred. Thus, to be prepared, you must visualize a war for survival. I will take you to Armageddon and back. I have been there, and I have worked with managers who have been there. Sam Walton was there in 1950 when his small chain of Ben Franklin stores closed. William Y. Tauscher was there in 1978 when he discovered that Lag Drug Company, the forerunner of FoxMeyer Corporation, was bankrupt. John Lewis was there in 1980 when Amdahl Corporation's IBM plug-compatible, mainframe computers were infested with so many bugs that customers were demanding refunds. And I was there in 1978 when the FoxMeyer venture capitalists blind-sided me into near financial devastation and again in 1986 when a frightened bank obtained a writ of attachment on my bank accounts. Know this: Those who are prepared for crisis not only survive; they thrive.

* Sun Tzu, *The Art of War*, p. 41.

Sam Walton bounced back to build Wal-Mart Stores and a megabillion dollar fortune. Bill Tauscher rebounded by building FoxMeyer Corporation into the second largest drug, health, and beauty aids distributor in the country, with sales of $3 billion. Tauscher sold FoxMeyer Corporation in 1986 for $350 million, and in 1987 he acquired control of Computerland. John Lewis saved Amdahl Corporation with an injection of supplier capital and a commitment to exhaustive, pre-rollout testing of all products. My firm bounced back (twice) from financial devastation to become one of the most effective workout, turn-around, and start-up investment banking firms in the country.

Survival requires avoiding denial. If you feel uncertain about the economy, your region, your industry, or the efficacy of your company's technology, then you are experiencing a stressor event. Deny the signals, and you are dead. Treat the murmurs and whispers with a "no problem" disdain, and you are dead. Go to fancy power breakfasts with those who would idolize you when you should be crisis-formulating, and you are dead. In fact, if you treat these times with anything short of planning for all-out war, you will not have a company to worry about. You don't agree? Just remember: no business ever failed because it was overprepared. Face it, sooner or later, things are going to get rough, and you need ammunition; this book can keep your company alive. Make a four-inch-square box in your diary with a red pen. Every day, beginning today, write three things in the box that you will do to prepare for a sudden downturn in sales or a liquidity crisis. Then do those three things before the day ends. For today's insert write: (1) work accounts receivable harder; (2) terminate that one employee whose lack of results has been bugging you; (3) delay supplier's payments one week. You will see many more ideas for diary entries throughout the book, but begin acting today.

GENERIC DISASTERS

One of four kinds of disaster is likely to strike your business within the near future. You are probably not ready for any of them—most managers never are. The four generic crises are

- Product obsolescence
- Regional disaster
- Industry downturn
- National recession, depression, or runaway inflation

Let's talk about how your present uncertainty can alert you to each of these four generic crises and make you ready to face them.

Product Obsolescence

There are numerous examples of companies being broken on the rack by product obsolescence, but the one most thoroughly exposed in published documents is that of Itel Corporation.* A less well-known and altogether happier story is that of Moldex/ Metric. Each company faced a crisis due to product obsolescence—one survived.

ITEL CORPORATION   Itel was founded in 1967, and its primary business was purchasing IBM 360 computers and leasing them to others under two- to five-year operating leases, which were cancellable on 12 months' notice. Initial financing included a $10 million investment by Fireman's Fund Insurance Company (later acquired by American Express), a bank credit line of $105 million made available through Bank of America, and an initial public offering of Itel's common stock in October 1968. In 1969 the company earned $3 million on revenues of $40 million, which grew in ten years to adjusted earnings of $48.4 million on revenues of $688.7 million. There were "infirmities in the structure of Itel, its business, management, and professional support, which led to its collapse."** On January 19, 1981, Itel filed for protection under Chapter XI of the Bank-

---

* I recommend that you order a copy of the 352-page *Examiner's Report,* pertaining to Itel Corporation, United States Bankruptcy Court, Northern District of California, March 1981; from the Examiner, Munger, Tolles & Rickerhauser; 612 Flower Street; Los Angeles, CA 90017.
** References to people, events, and financial information concerning Itel Corporation are taken from the *Examiner's Report.*

ruptcy Act, resulting in hundreds of millions of dollars in losses to its public stockholders. The *Examiner's Report* cites several reasons for the fall of Itel, but its failure was precipitated by IBM's introduction of new computers in 1977 and by the simultaneous cancellation of lease insurance by Lloyd's of London. Itel's senior management had wisely diversified into marketing computers through its Data Products Group, which had achieved revenues of $170 million by 1977. But when Itel senior management turned to that division for cash flow, it came up empty. What happened?

The Data Products Group's "inventory records in 1978 were in shambles."* The records did not reflect the group's inventory, its location, or its condition. The company's internal auditor believed Data Products Group's inventory was grossly overstated, and he recommended a reserve of $8 million to $13 million. Even though Itel was a publicly held corporation, managers of the Data Products Group reported the overstated inventory to senior management, which made erroneous filings with the Securities and Exchange Commission. Moreover, the group's basic management information system, which was supposed to control billings and receivables, was inefficient. Although overblown financial statements were given willy-nilly to stockholders, lenders, and investors, Data Products Group management knew that their numbers were inadequate and that the division would crash the following year.

While the crisis was swept under the rug, Itel maintained its lavish lifestyle. "Persian rugs on the floors and Perrier water in the office refrigerators greeted visitors to Itel's San Francisco headquarters at One Embarcadero Center. Executives, successful salespeople, and deal prospects were ferried about the country in a company jet airplane. The successful Itel performers, in addition to high compensation, were invited to the annual meetings of the 'Itel Club' and entertained and motivated during a shipboard cruise or a week's stay at a first-class resort."**

A more appropriate response to Itel's losing its computer-

---

* *Examiner's Report*
** *Examiner's Report*

leasing business and relying on its Data Products Group would have been a recognition of the bloated inventory records, a downsizing and refocusing of the business, a termination of the "no problem" guys who ran the division, and a public recanting of the errors in Data Products Group's financial reporting. Apple Computer Corporation and others have survived product obsolescence problems via changes in both management and operating methods. But, that is not what occurred at Itel.

According to the *Examiner's Report,* incompetence at Itel was only one facet of management's character; there was another, more serious flaw. Members of Itel's management team "were aware near the end of 1978 that Itel's computer-leasing business was in serious difficulty and that Itel's computer-sales business was slowing and was threatened by new IBM technology."* With this knowledge, Itel's senior management—Peter S. Redfield, John H. Clark, and Joe D. Foster—sold thousands of shares of Itel stock to the public at prices ranging from $26 to $32.50 per share (the stock later fell to less than $1 per share). The *Examiner's Report* stated that such a sale was probably a violation of Section 10(b)5 of the Securities Exchange Act and that it could result in fines and imprisonment. Itel's management has gone unpunished.

After filing for bankruptcy protection and settling with creditors, Itel (under more enlightened management) has rebounded, becoming a highly successful and diversified company. Its crash, as explicated in the *Examiner's Report,* is a classic example of corporate murder by a management unprepared to address its problems head-on and thus unprepared to protect its shareholders.

MOLDEX/METRIC   In contrast, Herbert Magdison, president of Moldex/Metric, addressed his company's product obsolescence with readiness and intelligence, and he came out of it with his integrity intact. Moldex/Metric grew to sales of $60 million over twenty years of manufacturing molded bra cups for such swimwear makers as Jantzen and for such foundation-garment makers as International Playtex. But fashions—and fortunes—

* *Examiner's Report*

change. By the late 1970s, big busts were out, and foundation-wear companies began making bra cups in-house.

Magdison recognized that he desperately needed a new product. Through problem formulation and opportunity analysis, he found it: disposable face masks for industrial workers. Against bracing competition from 3M Corporation, which dominates the $75 million mask market, Moldex went after the higher end of the market—a 75-cent mask versus 3M's 65-cent model—and offered greater durability and comfort. The Moldex mask features a plastic mesh that holds the mask's shape, a cross between the old bra cups and a fighter pilot's mask.

By 1987, Moldex/Metric had captured 10 percent of the disposable face-mask market, and with a related safety product (foam earplugs), its sales grew to $265 million. Magdison, who was 29 when the hammer fell, met the enemy of obsolescence head-on, with the happy result that Moldex/Metric is four times larger and more profitable than it was before the cup crisis.*

Thus, at the same time, two companies in the same state were drawn onto the battlefield by that devilish enemy, product obsolescence. One management team denied the problem, presented false financial statements to the public in order to support its stock price (which is more than mere denial), and then dumped shares on an unsuspecting public by using insider information. The other management team was forthright, identified its crisis as potentially devastating, and found new products for its technological capability as well as a market segment that it could conquer.

DON'T JUMP! The apparel industry, centered on Seventh Avenue, has witnessed thousands of business failures due to product obsolescence. If a garment manufacturer believes short hemlines will come back when, in fact, customers prefer a midcalf look, there is no way to get rid of twelve thousand miniskirts except via a bankruptcy and liquidation. As a result of living for so many years with the noose of product obsoles-

* *Forbes* (April 20, 1987), p. 105.

cence dangling over their heads, Seventh Avenue businesspeople have developed a gallows humor.

The late Myron Cohen told the story of Jacob and Sam, two partners who manufactured women's dresses on the twelfth floor of a building on Seventh Avenue. Their arch competitors were on the sixth floor of the same building. Every year for twenty-five years, the two companies competed viciously to predict the trend in women's dresses for the upcoming season. Their designs were closely held secrets, and the fabrics they selected were even more closely guarded. But the sixth floor company outsmarted Jacob and Sam year after year.

Finally, the partners were wiped out. Jacob walked over to their factory's twelfth-floor window, flung it open, and climbed out onto the ledge.

"This is it, Sammy. I can't take another bankruptcy," said Jacob.

"Don't do it!" Sam said, as he rushed to the window in shock and disbelief. "Let's give it one more season."

"No, Sammy. I'm going to jump," said Jacob.

And he did.

As Jacob fell, he looked into the window of the sixth floor and got a glimpse of the competition.

Jacob looked up, saw Sam at the window, and yelled to him, "Cut velvet!"

The gallows humor of Seventh Avenue suggests that it is never too late to implement a plan to avoid the crisis of product obsolescence—there are always six more flights, time enough to think up a solution. However, if you plan ahead more cautiously than Jacob did, you will survive to see the results of your labor. Rather than arriving at a solution during a free-fall, gather your team into the conference room (as I suggest in Chapter 2), and begin crisis-formulating.

Regional Disasters

The murmurs and whispers you hear could be the early warnings of a regional downturn. A major employer in the community could go under. The local subsidiary of a manufacturing plant employing twenty thousand people could be closed as a result of foreign competition. A large employer in your region could shut down as a result of the takeover of its parent. A local chemical processor could be closed for environmental reasons, such as the contamination incident in Bhopal. The President could ban sales to Eastern Europe of a product that your region produces, such as President Carter did in the late 1970s, to the dismay of thousands of farmers. If your region is dominated by one large company, its indigestion could give your company a stomach ulcer. Your company may do 40 percent of its business with a local manufacturer that decides to manufacture overseas, and if its doors are padlocked, what do you do to survive? How do you avoid a West Texas scenario? There is one answer to all of these scenarios. You become ready—before the freefall. You learn crisis-intervention, and you develop a redirect-and-grow plan. I will show you how to do all of these things.

"How can you tell the difference between a Texas oil man and a pigeon?" asked my friend from Austin. "A pigeon can still make a deposit on a Mercedes." That is how bad it got when the oil disaster struck Texas in the early 1980s. I will show you in Chapter 3 how John Madden, president of Rex Engineering, used the crisis in the oil industry to find new opportunities for his company, which distributed oil field equipment. But for now, let us examine what a regional disaster could look like.

Española, New Mexico, has a population of twelve thousand, is located between Santa Fe and Taos, and is the center of a car-modifying cult known as "low-riders." (For those of us with unmodified cars, it can be startling to see a restored, repainted 1957 Chevrolet that's riding three inches off the ground suddenly raise its back end and, through some invisible hydraulic mechanism, rock its backside like the buttocks of a well-built woman.) Española is a financial South Bronx, offering virtually no job opportunities and no hope to its unemployed, largely Hispanic population. Its inhabitants work outside of town, and they spend their income there as well. The town is the butt of insipidly bad jokes. Española is an economic disaster—a full-fledged crisis.

However, to Española's bright, energetic young mayor,

Richard Lucero, the town is an opportunity. With commercial and industrial space renting for as low as 10 cents per square foot per month, and with a community college turning out young people with skills, a manufacturer in the Southern Rockies has to consider Española. Thus, Lucero recently created a fifty-acre industrial park between Española and Los Alamos, and he has plans for a fourteen-acre downtown cultural and retail mall along the lines of South Street Seaport in New York City.

Think of this little town with its low-riders and its 10-cents-per-square-foot rentals when you are contemplating the effects of a regional disaster. Twenty percent unemployment is not a horror to Mayor Lucero—it would be a godsend. It would also be an improvement in some communities in West Texas, along the Mississippi Delta in Louisiana, and in northern New Mexico where joblessness is the enemy.

It could happen in your community. You should forecast the effects of a disaster of this magnitude and, as Mayor Lucero is doing, "make much of the negatives." Use inexpensive, job-creational, federal, long-term/low-interest-rate loans and grants (see Chapter 5), and lure the employers back with a tourist industry and small manufacturers. Low rents, tax abatement, and a young work force are the positives that one can use for the brick and mortar.

In Belmont County, Ohio, across the river from Wheeling, West Virginia, the mining industry died twenty years ago. But a young economic development officer, Steven Weir, can pull $5 million together from Ohio state and federal programs faster than than you can say, "Where can I find money?" Crisis is a way of life in some parts of the country, and it is in these remote valleys of unemployment that you will find financial virtuosos who can orchestrate an economic rebirth.

The key to bootstrapping in a regional disaster is not to deny the problem. As Sun Tzu wrote, to win the war one must get inside the mind of the opponent. Here the opponent is lack of business activity. If you can modify the opinions that people have about your community, you can build on what is perceived as a disaster. To deny a regional disaster and hold the belief that things will get better is to permit the problem to become far worse. Crisis intervention techniques are discussed in Chapter 2.

Industry Downturn

All of us know a handful of industries that have been ailing and sickly during the last few years. Look at Wall Street for the most recent saga of cancer of the billfold. Wall Street is the perfect example of a service industry setting aside the things it does best (servicing clients) and going hell-bent-for-leather into selling products (junk bonds, portfolio insurance, and programmed trading), making money hand over fist and ignoring the fact that the patient may soon go into shock.

But the shock on Wall Street will pale by comparison to what will happen in health care. Physicians may have money running out of their eyes, ears, noses, and billfolds right now, but the $430 billion health-care industry is about to collapse. There are enough signs of uncertainty in this field today that if you were to put each sign on an X-ray film and line them up end to end, the film would stretch from the Mayo Clinic to Johns Hopkins University.

The nation's health-care costs are rising dramatically without a concomitant improvement in the health of its citizens. Health-care expenditures in the United States exceed $430 billion per annum, or 11 percent of the GNP. Health insurance rates for traditional idemnity insurers and health maintenance organizations (HMOs) increased by more than 20 percent from 1986 to 1987. Physicians' fees increased 6 percent in 1986. Prescription drug prices increased 9 percent in 1986 and 6.8 percent for the first half of 1987. The costs of treating people who suffer some form of mental illness is increasing at a rate of 10 to 25 percent per annum in the 1980s, and mental health problems now account for 30 percent of an employer's total health-care costs.

The rising cost of medical care might be justifiable if the mortality rate were declining. But that is not the case. Mortality rates are rising at about one-half the rate of health-care costs. The RAND Corporation recently reported that 32 percent of certain surgeries—coronary angiograms and upper-gastrointestinal tract endoscopies—are unnecessary.* Thirty-six percent of all diseases, according to the *New England Journal of Medicine,* are iatrogenic; that is, caused by medical treatment. Stated more precisely, we are paying more and getting less.

Would you run your business this way? If you underwrote the nation's health-care costs, would you allow physicians to perform unnecessary procedures simply because they are reimbursable? Would you pay physicians for services that are not tied to results? Would you permit physicians to upgrade diagnoses without checks or balances? Would you permit the prescription of drugs without proper assessment of their validity? How has the U.S. medical industry been permitted to get so far out of hand?

One answer is the myth of high technology. Physicians can select from a battery of approximately fifteen hundred tests, many of them performed with a dizzying array of technologies. More than ten billion diagnostic tests are performed annually in the United States, costing nearly $150 billion per annum, or roughly one-third of the nation's annual health-care bill, yet one in seven test results reported to physicians from laboratories is either in error or unreliable. And still, health insurance pays for any tests prescribed by any physician.

Another reason for rising mortality and medical costs is that the typical American physician tests for and treats the symptoms of disease rather than the cause. The patient presents symptoms to the doctor who does not immediately recognize the disorder—nor does this doctor explore psychological or nutritional factors that may be contributing to the illness. "Rather, he repeatedly pursues organic possibilities through multiple tests, procedures, medications, and operations.... The dollar costs of this strategy are only exceeded by its potential for iatrogenic harm."**

EARLY WARNING SIGNS In October 1987, the Federal Health Care Financing Administration, which runs the Medicare pro-

---

* *Healthweek* (November 23, 1987), p. 2.
** *Journal of the American Medical Association* 254 (21) (December 6, 1985), p. 3075.

gram, said it will propose a plan to Congress by year's end to identify doctors who order too many tests. The goal is to steer the thirty-one million Medicare beneficiaries away from these doctors. Seventy-five percent of physicians queried by the American Medical Association admitted that they overtest, blaming the need for "defensive" medicine to protect themselves from malpractice suits. Yet some tests actually cause death: researchers at the University of Massachusetts found that of heart attack victims who have a pulmonary artery catheter (inserted to monitor blood pressure and flow), twice as many die as those who do not have the device. Some tests are fraudulent: cytotoxic tests that reputedly identify allergies, "submaximal" levels of vitamins, and low bone density are suspect.* And some tests are unreliable: Congress's Office of Technology Assessment recently found that nine out of ten AIDS tests showing negative—that is, no AIDS—were in error.

There are many flashing yellow lights warning the health-care industry of a pending change in their pricing system. But are health-care providers beginning to get ready for a doomsday scenario? Not at all.

PRESCRIPTION How should a clinic, hospital, pharmaceutical company, or test equipment manufacturer respond to these warning signals? They should forecast the effects of downsizing the medical reimbursement system. This will surely mean both changes in the method of treating patients and smaller fees. Once the effects of the crisis have been forecast, health-care providers should conserve cash, buy time, cut costs, and lay off inefficient people. When they are lean and mean, they should develop and implement a redirect-and-grow plan, as set forth in Chapter 12.

National Recession, Depression, or Runaway Inflation

What if all of the first three generic disasters erupt in the middle of an earth-shaking national recession, depression, or runaway

* *U.S. News & World Report* (November 23, 1987), p. 68.

inflation? Your company must be ready for the "big one."

On October 19, 1987, commonly referred to as Black Monday, the Dow Jones Industrial Average fell 508 points. This was mainly a response to the danger signals from international economies and overextended financial institutions. Perhaps the worst signal of all was not the stock market's decline but the federal government's response. On Tuesday morning, it flooded the investment banks with cash, rather than witness their bankruptcies. Unbridled, senseless greed was not punished. Off-the-shelf junk bonds were created to fit any size takeover, and takeovers were generated by the investment banks because the product could be sold. Goodbye to the service aspect of investment banking. Greed, thy name is junk-bond takeover.

How long will the government continue to reward Wall Street's feckless behavior? It seems forever. Yet to do so is inflationary and merely causes the impending jolt to hit us that much harder. As Warren Buffet told the followers of Benjamin Graham at their bi-annual meeting in Williamsburg, Virginia (coincidentally on Black Monday), "You know something is really wrong when a person can open a savings and loan and give out government insurance chits to its depositors while investing in anything he wants."

Nor can we ignore the trembling ground on which our commercial banks are standing. Our largest banks have loaned over $5 billion to each of a large number of foreign countries who are unable to repay these loans. When the banks deal with this problem, several will go out of business (or perhaps be saved by the government—which will intensify the inflation scenario), and millions of other loans will be called. All of us will experience a shutdown at the loan window, except at interest rates of 20 percent or more.

WHAT HAPPENED TO ACCOUNTABILITY?   You can be fairly certain that we are headed for hard times when accountability is not given the respect it deserves. If greed is underwritten by the federal government, if bad business judgments and resultant losses are treated by Uncle Sam with monetary transfusions, then someone will have to pay the bill. That someone is your business and mine, and the price we will pay is either inflation or recession or both.

WHAT IS WRONG WITH THE ECONOMY?   At least three significant factors could tumble the United States economy into a serious recession: (1) the general meltdown of the financial markets when the investment banking system, during a sharp sell-off brought on by real economic or political forces, proves unable to supply capital; (2) the increased savings and concomitant deferral of purchases by consumers, with resulting factory shutdowns and layoffs; or (3) the foreign influence on our economy, which will be seen when Japanese, West German, and other foreign institutions pass on a few treasury bill auctions.

We have been living for several years on a fault line created by an obsessive devotion to high-stakes, financial maneuvering as a shortcut to wealth—the "casino society," as *Business Week* named it in July 1987. The volume of securities market transactions in the United States, Europe, Hong Kong, and Japan had soared beyond economic purpose through mid-1987, which overburdened an inadequately capitalized financial system. Had not the Federal Reserve system pumped money into the money-market banks on Tuesday morning, October 20, 1987, financial markets throughout the world would have collapsed. The financial "meltdown" (as John J. Phelan, chairman of the New York Stock Exchange, called October 19) occurred "in the absence of any true calamity," reported the *Wall Street Journal.* So, the *Journal* asks, "What might happen to the markets in a major political or economic crisis?" The answer is that a real meltdown could happen, and it could happen tomorrow morning. How will the country respond?

People react to uncertainty by becoming liquid, genuinely liquid. We save money and defer purchases. In countries whose citizens have experienced war, economic volatility, or political oppression within the last two generations, the savings rate is considerably higher than it is in the United States. In the United States, we save money at the rate of $9,733 per year per person. In West Germany, the savings rate is $12,288 per person, and in Japan, the rate is $27,303 per person. Watch what happens when Americans begin saving $2,000 more per person: half a trillion dollars will be removed from the gross national product. The industries most affected will be housing, automobiles, travel, and apparel—the producers of large ticket items sold to consumers—and this will affect all of us. In 1986 these industries accounted for over $1 trillion in shipments (factory prices) and thirteen million jobs.* If half of the new savings is pulled out of these four industries across the board, they will decline by 25 percent, or $250 billion. More than three million people will be laid off, and the "horror" will spread to all sectors with corresponding results.

In addition, Japanese and West Germans can cause a calamity in the U.S. economy by withholding their purchases of American securities and products. Americans have made themselves hostages of the Japanese, West Germans, and Koreans by buying their cars, VCRs, and TVs. Because foreign investors are presently the principal buyers of U.S. government notes and corporate bonds, should they withdraw their support, interest rates would rise, as would prices of goods and services, and the factory shutdowns, layoffs, and business failures would begin in earnest. Would our good friends the Japanese and West Germans do this? Sure they would. If they decided not to bid in the next treasury auction, that would drive the dollar down so that the Japanese and West Germans could come back into the market later and buy higher yields with cheaper dollars. Are they likely to do it? Nobody knows. These are the uncertainties with which we live.

Indeed, all of these scenarios could happen in tandem or sequentially. Per capita savings could rise, foreign investors could withdraw from buying U.S. government securities, sales of large consumer products could fall sharply, unemployment could rise, and interest rates could leap into the teens. In that event the fault line we are living on will open and those unprepared will tumble into the abyss.

"Prepare for death, if here at night you roam," wrote Dr. Samuel Johnson. We must avoid stumbling blindly into the abyss. Those of us who must go out every day and make a living

---

* U.S. Industrial Outlook 1987 (Washington, D.C.: U.S. Department of Commerce).

should indeed prepare ourselves for the terrible times caused by a monetary crisis.

THE BIGGEST PEBBLE IN OUR SHOE   Of the three scenarios, the one that most concerns Americans is the foreign-induced recession. Men and women in business are biting their finger-nails like hostages awaiting the death knell from their jailers. Although we have recently experienced recessions caused by consumer deferrals (1981) and a breakdown in our financial markets—the Federal Reserve interceded in both instances with instantaneous, easy money policies—we have no experience with a recession orchestrated by foreign powers. But look at the facts. Worldwide equity capitalization soared to $5.6 trillion at the end of 1986, from $1.5 trillion in 1975. But the U.S. market share shrank to 39.2 percent from 61.2 percent over the same period.* The Japanese market share grew to 31.8 percent from 12.3 percent between 1975 and 1986. U.S. corporations and the federal government have turned to foreign markets to raise capital at an alarming rate: $367 billion was raised abroad by American corporate and governmental borrowers in 1986, ver-sus $176 billion in 1982, and most of the borrowing was done in Japan.

United States investment bankers have used electronic and telecommunication systems (many imported from Japan) to create derivate financial instruments such as options and finan-cial futures markets, which bear about as much relationship to raising money for U.S. corporations as gambling in Las Vegas casinos bears to investing in worthy companies. Trading in financial futures and options aggregated $655.4 billion in 1986, compared with $81 billion in 1980. Look at it this way, America no longer holds the biggest poker games in its house, dragging a dime from each pot to invest in beer and pretzels. Rather than competing to get the games back into its own house, America is busy across the street, devising side-betting schemes to make a few bucks on the action. This is not the value-added role we expect of our investment bankers. If the trend continues, Amer-ican industry and the federal government will be in hock to the

* *Financial Times* (July 21, 1987), p. 2.

Japanese and West Germans, and if these foreign houses suddenly stop lending, or if they begin foreclosing on loans, America can kiss economic growth goodbye.

"It can't happen," you say. Let me point out two things. First, foreign banks and investors have bad debt reserves and margin requirements radically different from their American counterparts. Foreign governments are much more active as corporate lenders than is the United States government. Foreign corporations and banks are more highly leveraged than are their American counterparts. Consequently, foreign investors are buying securities from U.S. issuers with borrowed funds. This is scary.

Second, according to the *Wall Street Journal,* on Tuesday morning, October 20, 1987, when Wall Street's largest investment firms telephoned their banks to borrow desperately needed money, "Japanese banks threatened to stop lending." This is frightening. The future of the country has been mortgaged by the sale of securities to foreign lenders whose actions and reactions to our needs we neither understand nor have the ability to control. If they sneeze, we will catch pneumonia. This is the magnitude of the uncertainty.

While Wall Street forgets it is in the service business and devotes most of its time to creating products—junk bonds, financial futures, options, and portfolio insurance—and, worse still, begins tying up its capital with leveraged buy-outs of large corporations, government and corporate borrowers must necessarily look to international securities markets to raise money. This is the hostage scenario most likely to cause the economic calamity that most of us now fear. This scenario produces the questions of *when* and *how bad*—questions that are too frightening for some of us to ask.

WHEN WILL THE BOTTOM DROP, AND WHAT EFFECTS WILL IT HAVE?

The crash can occur any day. It will bankrupt the financial institutions first, because they are the most highly leveraged and because they employ a large number of inexperienced, overpaid young men and women. One-fourth of Wall Street's 260,000 employees hold MBA degrees, the validity of which piece of parchment will be severely tested in the crash. You can forget degrees in a crisis; business schools do not teach crisis management.

Immediately following the *second* Black Monday, corporations that need capital will fail, banks that loan money to Wall Street will be awash in bad debt and will call in loans to raise cash, and loan windows will begin to slam shut throughout the country. This is the most likely crisis scenario.

To survive in turbulent times, one must make *fearless* business decisions. I do not mean tough, nor do I mean strong. I mean fearless, as in standing before the abyss and making the tough calls to avoid falling in and pulling your company in on top of you. I can tell you how this is done because, for the last twenty years, all of my working hours have been devoted to helping men and women save their businesses when the bottom drops.

Fearlessness in Action

In the 1975-76 recession, when the prime rate reached 21 percent, I worked with Roger Main to raise $750,000 for IEC Electronics Corporation, Newark, New York. A contract manufacturer of semiconductor-based consumer electronic products, IEC Electronics is today one of *Business Week*'s one hundred greatest small companies, with sales of $24 million and net profits of $2.4 million. But it took the balls-to-the-wall toughness of Roger Main to pull his company through a very cruel period, a time when he could count the number of faithful friends on the fingers of one hand.

In the same recession, I found $1.5 million for ActMedia, which today is one of *Forbes*'s two hundred best small companies. ActMedia sells advertising space on supermarket shopping carts to consumer products advertisers. Bruce Failing, Jr., was in trouble with ActMedia's investors because sales dropped off the chart the year immediately following the financing, and he was booted out by an angry cadre of venture capitalists. With true grit and by aligning himself with overstretched suppliers, Failing regained control of the company. One of my most vivid memories from this period is of a foot race between Failing and one of the investors to reach ActMedia's bank and to get control of the cash—Failing won. Shortly thereafter, sales turned up, and the company bought out the investors at twice their cost. (Had they stayed in, investors would have made thirty times their money.) In 1986, ActMedia's sales were $35 million, on which it earned $4.6 million.

In 1978, I was with William Y. Tauscher and his former banker Richard H. Bard when they took control of the $80 million (sales) Lag Drug Company only to find it hopelessly insolvent. They used the carcass of a dead pharmaceutical distributor to acquire a healthy distributor of the same size— Fox-Vliet. Tauscher, Bard, and I persuaded dozens of Lag's suppliers that their only hope for collecting $12 million from Lag was to permit the purchase of Fox-Vliet. I raised $4.6 million for Tauscher and Bard to buy Fox-Vliet, and they nurtured FoxMeyer Corporation to $2.4 billion in sales. They acquired Ben Franklin Stores and Coast to Coast along the way, and in 1987, they acquired Computerland Corporation.

Do Not Fear a Crisis

Not only is it possible but it should also be one's goal to use a difficult period to pole-vault to a higher level of achievement. Crises are meant to be springboards for success. Never enter a period of uncertainty or crisis by fearing for your survival; rather, plan to come out of it better off than when you entered it. The Chinese word for crisis, "Wei-Ji," is made up of two characters. The first means danger; the second, opportunity. *Fortunes are made in hard times and lost in good times.* Or, as Nietzsche put it, "You must be a chaos to give birth to a rising star."

The key to success in hard times is achieving genuine liquidity. We may be entering a deep recession, and customers, lenders, suppliers, and investors are responding to uncertainty with unpredictable behavior. Very soon all of us will be conducting business during violent restructuring of capital markets, massive layoffs, radical corporate downsizing, extremely high interest rates, and reduced consumer spending. The U.S. economy is going to return to basics. Paper wealth will blow away; "dynamic hedging" will become Wall Street's Edsel. And soaring above the ashes of this unstable period will be businesspeople who learn how to hold their companies' heads above water when the bottom drops.

What did Black Monday tell us? That the economy is in trouble; that the Federal government has forgotten the meaning of accountability, which could be inflationary; that the U.S. economy is being held hostage by the Japanese and the West Germans, which could be recessionary; and that the commercial banking industry has loaned billions of dollars to weak and troubled countries, the write-off of which could mean illiquidity for all of our businesses. These are the causes of the present turbulence. What does it mean for our businesses? It means that we have to treat the forthcoming economic crisis, in whatever form it takes, as a factor in our companies' near-term plans and take appropriate steps.

SUMMARY

Display the following thoughts on your wall where they will be highly visible.

1. Signals of pending trouble
   a. *Feckless behavior and runaway greed among financial institutions.* When a service industry that controls the nation's cash becomes enthralled with selling products instead of serving clients, you can be sure we are near the top of a business cycle because the basics have been forgotten.
   b. *Per capita savings in the United States.* Read the business journals regularly, and keep a sharp eye out for this indicator. When it begins to rise in a full-employment economy, jobs will be cut.
   c. *Being held hostage by foreign investors.* No amount of government jaw-boning can influence the billions

of dollars that West German and Japanese investors have gained from selling us cars, computers, VCRs, and television sets. Money seeks the highest, safest yield it can find, and that yield is U.S. government and corporate bonds. Why wouldn't foreign investors pass up a few Treasury auctions in order to buy higher yields with cheaper dollars later on? Watch for signs of the U.S. Government having difficulty selling its debt.

   d. *Government accountability.* We have a new administration in place in 1989. Will it introduce the concept of accountability to the investment banking industry when the next Black Monday strikes? Or will it reward Wall Street's greed with easy credit? Will the commercial banking industry be permitted to treat bad debt from third world countries as if it were good? Will Medicare, Medicaid, and private health care insurers continue to pass on the higher costs of health-care delivery to industry and labor unions? If the answer is "No!" and the new administration decides to wear the white hat of a first-term presidency by bringing the word accountability back into the lexicon of Washington, you will see the sudden downsizing of three huge industries: investment banking, commercial banking, and health-care delivery.

2. Four crisis scenarios
   a. *Product obsolescence.* If your company is selling a product or providing a service to financial institutions, health-care providers, capital intensive manufacturers, or consumers, your product or service may become obsolete very quickly. You would be well advised either to begin developing products or services for other markets or to begin developing much less expensive products or services for your present customers. It is time to think of five to ten other sources of cash flow, because you are going to need them. Is there a division you can spin off to generate cash? Do it now. Is a rust-belt state luring you with cheap dollars to begin a development facility in an abandoned steel-fabricating plant? Do it now.

b. *Regional disaster.* What would your community be like with 25 percent unemployment? Could it take the hit? Are there support systems in place? Forget Economic Development Administration Disaster loans; forget Federal Deposit Insurance Agency bail-outs; forget any help from Washington. A new administration will likely turn its back on your region because of the new-broom-sweeps-clean dictum. Quietly call the other chief executive offices of the region together for a doomsday planning session. Do some forecasting of the degree of turbulence that could strike the area. Encourage a frank analysis of the strengths and weaknesses of the region. Then begin seeking emergency measures—not placebos, but solid, well-built underpinnings. Perhaps every company could agree to invest 5 percent of its pension fund into a regional work-out company, to be used to support critical local employers caught unprepared. Readiness can blunt the force of the blow.

c. *Industry downturn.* The pending economic crisis could hit your industry hard. Have you properly forecasted this eventuality? Do you have a diversification idea that you could mobilize into a plan? Is there an acquisition you could make, perhaps of an export business in which the cheap dollar is a key element? Now is a good time to explore intelligent diversification steps to deemphasize your reliance on cash flow from your principal activity. Read the biographies of the pioneers of the U.S. automobile industry. General Motors, Ford, and Chrysler are not manufacturers of marine engines, refrigerators, and aerospace equipment because these products somehow relate to cars and trucks. On the contrary. The automobile giants diversified in order to save their companies at various critical times over the last fifty years. With leveraged buy-out financing techniques so well understood today, you can diversify without tying up cash.

d. *National recession, depression, or runaway inflation.* This is the horror—the worst of all the crises. A combination of the first three worst-case scenarios could produce a nationwide free-fall of companies, jobs, and liquidity. Picture a moneyless economy with bank failures, plant shutdowns, joblessness, and worthless investments. What can you do today to prevent the bankruptcy and liquidation of your business? You can forecast the services that your industry will require in a doomsday scenario—moving and storage, liquidation and auction services, barter, the purchase and sale of used equipment, security service and guards to prevent vandalism; and work-out and turn-around experience. If you are liquid you will be able to buy by the ton in a depression, store the goods in inexpensive warehouses, and sell by the piece when the economy turns around.

3. Step 'n Fetchit
   The great black comedic actor Step 'n Fetchit died a few years ago, but his hilarious encounters with Moms Mably and others live on to tell you what lies ahead of you in the remainder of this book, so I will quote:
   "First I'm gonna tell ya what I'm gonna tell ya. Then I'm gonna tell ya what I said I was gonna tell ya. Then I'm gonna tell ya what I done told ya."

Now, here's what I'm gonna tell ya.

(1) The greatest fortunes are made in hard times.
(2) You can use a crisis as a springboard to reach a higher level of financial success.
(3) For your company to survive a crisis, you must do the following things:
   • Forecast the effects of the crisis
   • Select the right war buddies
   • Create genuine liquidity
   • Buy time
   • Cut costs
   • Learn back-to-the-wall street-fight tactics
   • Create a redirect-and-grow plan
   • Implement your plan

Chapter Two

Forecasting and Dealing with the Effects of a Crisis

Uncertainty is a stressor. A *crisis* is a growth-promoting condition. You cannot solve problems when your company is under stress. But if you can forecast crisis situations, and convince your key people to role-play your company out of them, you will have created the springboard for great success.

As the chief executive officer, it is important that you act as the producer-director of your company's rehearsals for its forthcoming play, "Doomsday." You want to accomplish two things: (1) scripting the play—writing its beginning, middle, and end, and (2) selecting the actors who can best carry it off. As producer, you want to invest in the most realistic script and put your money behind the most convincing actors and actresses. As director, you want the script you have selected to come alive, to resonate with reality and poignancy, and you want your chosen actors and actresses to feel their roles, to reach inside themselves and find their hearts and emotions, because the roles they will act out will make or break the play.

The setting for the preproduction rehearsal of "Doomsday" is your company's conference room. The props are the conference-room table, the chairs, some legal pads and pencils, and a blackboard and chalk.

FORECASTING THE EFFECTS OF A CRISIS

Before you have called the actors and actresses into the conference room for their auditions, write on the board the four possible crisis scenarios:

- Product obsolescence
- Regional disaster
- Industry downturn
- National recession, depression, or runaway inflation

The likelihood of these four events occurring is the reason that you have decided to have a play, because you want to forecast the effects on your company of the coming battle (script of the play) and select your war buddies (the best actors and actresses). Do not alert your managers to the subject of the meeting; surprise is the key element of your overall plan.

Role-Play a Possible Crisis

Invite your key people into the conference room. Tell them you want to do some downside forecasting. Then ask them to sound out all of the things that could go wrong in their divisions. When you write them on the blackboard the list will appear something like the following.

MARKETING

1. Customers will send back shipments protesting that they never placed the orders.
2. Potential customers currently testing our newest products will fail to order them, claiming that they do not have sufficient information, that their budget has been cut, or that someone above them has scotched the project.
3. My top salesmen will leave us and join a competitor.
4. Customers will delay payments from thirty to sixty days; some will stretch them to ninety days.
5. Customers will demand a higher service component with each sale, more training of their personnel, a longer warranty, and other services.

PRODUCTION

1. Our principal suppliers may go out of business, and we do not have second sources lined up, or for components that are second-sourced, the suppliers may not be well capitalized or may be more expensive.
2. Certain suppliers may demand faster payments for critical components; if we do not maintain our payments on a current basis, they may put us on COD terms.
3. It is not far-fetched to project a decline in quality of the parts we are receiving if our suppliers cut back sharply either on their quality control or in other key areas.
4. A further decline in the value of the dollar could make the cost of our imported components prohibitively expensive.
5. We may have to lay off production workers, which could diminish our ability to produce or to maintain our quality standards.

HUMAN RESOURCES

1. The threat of strikes and work stoppages is our biggest fear. If we go into a lay-off period, we could be struck.
2. The threat of strikes due to reductions in our hourly wage rates is another nightmare.
3. Low morale due to the fear of recession, lay-offs, or reductions in wage rates is another possible problem.

TREASURY

1. Our bank could fail, the deposits we maintain could be tied up, and amounts above $20,000 could be seized by creditors.
2. Our bank officer could leave the bank or be relocated. He has been giving us instant credit on all deposits, rather than holding them for seven days. We could lose this favorable treatment if he leaves the bank.
3. Our bank could be acquired by a megabillion-dollar bank from another state, and we could become just a number. Employees' payroll checks may not be cashable, or we may lose other privileges if the bank is acquired.

CHIEF FINANCIAL OFFICER

1. Our investment banker could fail. Our access to capital markets could dry up.
2. Our stock price could fall, and although we may want to buy back our own stock, if the loan window shuts, we could be prey to a corporate raid.
3. Our expansion plans for the coming year require that we raise $10 million in fresh capital. Conventional sources of financing may disappear and leave us with a half-built plant and half-developed new products. If we cannot raise $10 million, our company could slide from being an industry leader to being just one of the pack.

Review the Actors' Performances

The scenarios that your key managers describe are stressors—verbalizations of their areas of potential vulnerability—not crises. You must decide whether these stressors are overwhelming the clear and effective thinking of your managers or whether your managers are describing possible downside situations for which they have devised solutions. Do your managers hear footsteps and react quickly to them? Or are they members of the "woe is me" school? Another danger is the "no problem" guys, the ones who do not sense any trouble on the horizon. A third danger is the manager who cannot cooperate with others.

Describe the four scenarios to your managers. Tell them you are concerned and that you want to get the company ready for trouble. Ask them whether they have effective strategies to deflect the nightmares that bother them. It is likely that your managers are unprepared, that they do not have effective strategies. Do you fire the ones who are not ready? It depends. There are three kinds of managers you will want to terminate: the "woe is me," the "no problem," and the "cannot cooperate" types. I will explain why momentarily, but let's reflect on Itel briefly.

Put yourself in the chief executive officer's chair at Itel when the double-whammy hit: IBM announces a new mainframe computer that will make obsolete hundreds of millions of dollars of computers that Itel has on operating leases, and

Lloyd's of London cancels the company's lease-insurance policy. You know that you must abandon the computer-leasing business, thus you look to the management of the Data Products Group to find strength. To your utter dismay, the division management has swept all of its problems under the rug, its books and records are in a sorry mess, and the management is too uncooperative to tell the board of directors the truth. An internal audit of Data Products Group's books and records reveals that the management of this $170 million (1977 revenues) division has been grossly overstating sales and inventory while grossly understating both the deterioration of its relationship with its computer supplier and the risks of competing with IBM, Digital Equipment, and other mainframe manufacturers. The internal audit report would be, in my opinion, grounds for termination of the Data Products Group management team. Truthful reporting, clarity in communications, and standing up to the problem in the division could have saved Itel. But the chief executive officer and the senior management of Itel chose to do just the opposite, which led to the collapse of the company, the loss of everyone's investment, and the corruption and eventual personal ruin of the people who reacted out of fear.

Show the "No Problem" Guys the Door

As you discuss the potential stressors with your key managers, asking them questions about their readiness, you will find some who will say "no problem." I cannot stress this enough: be very careful of these unrealistic types and get rid of them. If their values are permitted to permeate the organization so that no one stands up to say, "Hey! This could be serious," then by the time your problem is recognized, your company will be in a condition of crisis, too paralyzed to move. When this happens, the day-to-day activities of the company will become suffused with accusations, retaliations, general contentiousness, demoralization, and eventually ruin.

Sanford C. Sigoloff, 56, is the most widely known corporate turn-around expert in the country—Ampex, Daylin, and most recently Wickes, which filed the second largest bankruptcy ever in 1982. His first step in engineering work-outs is to look for his most loyal lieutenants. He does not want to hear "no problem" from middle managers. He wants details of their problems. Says Bruce Spector, a Los Angeles bankruptcy lawyer who worked on Wickes with Sigoloff: "It's the complexity. He's got to have it. His love is problem solving and synthesizing information. He lives on it."*

Not only had Sigoloff earned degrees in both physics and chemistry from UCLA, but in the early days of crisis intervention at Wickes, he called his managers together on Saturday mornings and floored them with the incredible amount of detail he had absorbed in his first thirty days as CEO. He knew the number of feet from the conveyor belt to the loading dock, whether there was a ladies' room on the first floor and how far it was from the elevators, and how many items were on the shelves. On a home computer, working far into the night, Sigoloff had produced cash-flow models. No detail failed to catch his eye or to find a cell in his memory bank. The managers could not hide the problems in their area of operations from Sigoloff, whose nickname is "Ming the Merciless."

To ease tensions among middle managers during the Daylin turn-around, Sigoloff gave names to the company's crises. Each one was called a "ticking time bomb," and he gave his managers mock bombs complete with alarm clocks. He also addressed their most urgent needs; for example, he rebalanced inventory to make certain the company could fill orders in order to make life bearable for the marketing managers while they carried out his instructions to lay off thousands of employees and sell every unnecessary asset for cash.

An Itel middle manager would have lasted a millisecond under a crisis-oriented CEO like Sigoloff. He is unrelenting with his managers in order to get all the problems on the table. The sign over Sigoloff's desk at Daylin read:

> When You Walk Through the Valley of the Shadow of Death, Remember This: I Am the Meanest Son of a Bitch in the Valley.

---

* *Fortune* (January 5, 1987), p. 105.

Toughness may not be your historical management style, and I am not encouraging you to adopt an uncomfortable persona. But you must get at the truth: you must be critical of your managers, you must be clear with them, and you must seek clarity from them in precrisis periods.

Unlike Sigoloff, Steven Kumble could not inspire confidence and loyalty among his managers at the law firm of Finley, Kumble, Wagner, Heine, Underberg, Manley & Carey, which he built in ten years to revenues of $165 million. By 1986, the 650 lawyers in Finley, Kumble's twelve offices across the country had formed warring fiefdoms, some offices refused to take telephone calls from others, and Kumble and another senior partner refused to speak to one another.

Kumble had attracted "rainmakers" to join the firm—ex-politicians such as Governor Hugh Carey of New York—who could bring in prestigious clients. But arguments quickly broke out between the partners over who had brought which client to the firm. At a regularly scheduled management meeting in Miami in February 1987, Kumble was voted out as senior managing partner, the Finley, Kumble law firm broke into pieces, and the company filed for protection under Chapter XI a year later.*

You will not be able to convince your managers to put all of their problems on the table unless you have inspired confidence, loyalty, and fairness. You must encourage candor. The emperor must be told he is not wearing clothes if that is the case. He must not behead the couriers who bring him bad news, nor must he delegate all of the difficult jobs—firings, plant closings, and litigations. Yet it is his responsibility to show that he will be merciless with any middle manager who does not bring him the unvarnished truth with complete details of his or her fears, problems, and uncertainties. He must then determine which of the managers will be his companions on the journey through the Valley of the Shadow of Death.

---

* *Forbes* (June 1, 1987), p. 124.

What Makes a Good Manager?

The principal personality characteristics that you should look for when selecting the company's lieutenants for the pending battle are the following:

- Heart: the drive that impels a person to make sacrifices to save the company
- The ability to cooperate: an understanding of the law of reciprocity, which binds the corps together even when individual tasks are different
- Courage: the internal strength to stand up to the most severe attacks without blinking or backing off
- An understanding of leverage: a second sense that (1) the short-term goals of the battle are to increase time, money, and supporters; and that (2) every resource must be leveraged to strengthen these three goals.

Much has been written about the personality characteristics of "winners," but let me add my thoughts about what makes a survivor.

HEART You will want to select lieutenants whose experiential background is one of serious deprivation. Perhaps they were raised in embarrassing poverty or with a childhood deprivation that prevented their playing with other children. Perhaps (like Richard Bard, number two to Bill Tauscher at FoxMeyer) they were raised in an orphanage. Whatever the deprivation, you want your war buddies to be driven to survive because not surviving—returning to that earlier time of deprivation—is too painful to contemplate.

People who were raised with safety nets seldom have heart. You cannot develop the will to overcome oppressive conditions unless you have the built-in drive that says "I must survive, and thrive, and succeed—I must do it with this company and in this circumstance because this is the precise situation that all the pain incurred in my childhood has trained me for. This company is my stage. I am its costar. This is my moment— my chance."

People with heart accept *all* of the responsibility for their decisions. They are fully accountable. They are not paralyzed by the fear of failure. They do not measure their achievements by outside standards—rather, they judge their success by how well they contribute to the company's goals, how well they handle change, how much confusion they cut through with clarity and vision, and how much joy and satisfaction they derive from winning the company's fight, whatever that fight may be.

People with heart always beat people without heart. The reason is quite simple. The people with heart know what drives the people without heart, but the people without heart never understand what drives the people with heart.

If you do not know the psychological makeup of your managers, if you do not know the deprivation in their childhoods or the drive of their hearts, now is a good time for a deep-down, close-to-the-bone private talk with them.

THE ABILITY TO COOPERATE The overriding, unspoken rule in business is trust—the knowledge inherent in all business people that they may meet again and that if a person has gone back on his word, he cannot be trusted the next time around. This is the Law of Reciprocity: Achievement is rewarded, failure is punished, and dishonesty results in banishment. Cooperation with members inside and outside the organization works when everyone understands the Law of Reciprocity.

The best way to ensure cooperation among your managers is to prepare a written statement of your company's survival mission very early. Clearly state the goals toward which you will be working and the moral code by which you will operate. If your goal is to take refuge in Chapter XI in order to buy time to implement a plan, make the statement clear to all. Ask your people to read this statement carefully. Tell them that they will be happy in the bleakest part of the battle only if they are focused on the mission and abide by the code of ethics. Clarity is vital to cooperation. People cannot cooperate with you unless they know exactly what you want from them and what you will not tolerate. Therefore, it is important to make yourself clear. Let others know what you expect of them and what they can expect from you.

The great enforcer of cooperation in the survival-oriented company is the continuing relationship. I have devised a test to see which buddies I want and which I do not want with me under battlefield conditions. Call one of your managers into the office, shut the door, and ask him to solve the following riddle.

He gets a telephone call from someone he does not know. He has never heard the voice before, and he cannot tell the age or the sex of the person calling. The voice says, "Every Monday night at midnight, you will bring a bag containing $1,000 in cash to a tree in Central Park. You will go and sit in your car for fifteen minutes. Then you will return to the tree where you will find a bag of diamonds (or gold, or baseball cards—whatever you fondly desire). Do not tell anyone. Do not try to see who leaves the diamonds. Do you agree to do this?"

The manager agrees. On the first Monday night he leaves the bag of money at the appointed tree at midnight, waits fifteen minutes, then returns and finds the sack of diamonds. On the second Monday night he leaves the bag of money, waits fifteen minutes, then returns and picks up the sack of diamonds. This is good. He likes it. On the third Monday night he leaves the bag of money, waits fifteen minutes, then returns—but there is no sack of diamonds.

"What would you do on the next Monday night?"

Look straight into the eyes of your manager when you ask this question. There are two wrong answers and one right one. The first wrong answer is, "I would drop off the money in a bag as usual and see if he leaves the diamonds." This is the response of a pleaser, a person who receives pleasure from putting the needs of others ahead of himself. He is saying, "You deceived me once, but I'm a victim most of the time anyway, so I'll let you hit me with two tits before I give you back a tat." This manager will not serve you well in a barrage of incoming missiles from lenders and creditors.

The second wrong answer is, "The son of a bitch screwed me once. I won't give him a second chance." This manager has too much anger. He is willing to forego the possibility of receiving future pleasure in order to deliver pain today to the person who disappointed him. He will take his ball and glove and leave the field carrying his honor like a badge of courage. Show this manager the employment pages of the *Wall Street Journal.*

The correct answer is, "I would return to the tree at 12:15 A.M. on the following Monday, and if I see the sack of diamonds he owes me, then on the Monday after that, I will leave my bag of money at midnight and renew the game." This is a person who understands cooperation. He played a perfect tit for tat; not two tits for a tat and not "game's over, you cheated!" He reciprocated in kind with the other player. This person will serve you well in a crisis. People will trust him, and you can trust him to carry out assignments on his own.

The cohesion of cooperation is not so strong in a bureaucratic corporation where the glue of stock ownership is a thin layer. There, many employees refuse to cooperate. They may, for example, take credit that is due a co-worker; they may sell their stock on insider information, as happened with Itel; or they might fail to reciprocate after another employee cooperates with them. Many "ivory tower" executives neglect to explain clearly what they expect from others in the organization, and the result of this lack of clarity is often a failure of cooperation or a misunderstanding about ethical standards. Confusion can result. At that point, the buddy you were counting on—frustrated and disappointed by the corporation—departs to join a company in which cooperation will always be reciprocated.

Masuru Ibuka and Akio Morita understood the importance of cooperation back in 1948 when they founded the SONY Corporation. They even wrote the words "mutual cooperation" into the original statement of their company's mission. As the years passed and the company grew, cooperation remained a priority and became recognized as a mark of SONY's operation. Ibuka and Morita cooperated with customers by providing top-quality products, and the customers reciprocated by paying higher prices for goods that carried the SONY name—the Law of Reciprocity in action.

COURAGE Your war buddies will need courage—not the physical sort that is expected of test pilots and submariners, but the courage of their convictions—moral courage. If your survival plan calls for an informal reorganization followed by a redirect-and-grow plan, as does the example I have selected in Chapter 12, then your company will lack the sue-proof safety net afforded by Chapter XI. As a result, you and your company are going to get sued quite a bit because your survival plan is unconventional—you want to preserve your creditors' and investors' values, rather than trash them by filing for bankruptcy protection.

Your largest creditors, who can afford the biggest law firms, will sue you for everything they can think of that you might have done. If your company has been unable to pay for a shipment of raw materials, your supplier's lawyer may cry "fraudulent inducement!" hoping that if your company is forced into bankruptcy, it can make the fraud charge stick and receive the full amount of the shipment plus interest and legal fees. Fraud claims are not dischargeable in bankruptcy.

There is no limit to the depths of deception and venality to which some law firms will descend in order to generate fees on behalf of a large client. Regrettably, law suits are public documents, and the local newspaper may have a stringer who sits in the courthouse copying the juicier lawsuits for publication the next morning. It takes courage to face the news of your company's lawsuits in the local papers or, worse yet, to see the story reprinted in the trade journals. We will discuss a strategy for leveraging litigation later on. Suffice it to say, it is primarily when your opponent is a lawyer that you will need to train your troops in back-to-the-wall street-fight tactics.

The mention of courage brings to mind the shipping entrepreneurs of earlier years. It must have taken enormous courage for a man to invest his life savings in a cargo that had a good chance of sinking to the bottom of the sea or of being seized by pirates. But the early merchants had that kind of courage, and as a result, they became wealthy while providing the goods that other people needed and wanted.

Cecilia Danieli of Italy provides a more contemporary example of that kind of courage. When she assumed control of the Danieli Company in 1980, the construction firm was in serious financial trouble. It had suffered losses of 1.7 billion lire ($1 million), and profit margins were getting thinner and thinner on large construction jobs. She took three bold and courageous steps and, by doing so, not only saved the company but turned it into an enterprise that did $200 million in sales in 1985.

Her first step was to rewrite the company's business plan, a move that meant rethinking the very bases on which the Danieli Company was built. Once that was done, she began bidding on midsize projects only, eschewing the huge jobs. She also put her company's energy into turnkey projects, in which it became responsible for designing, managing, and commissioning entire factories. The third step in her strategy was to move boldly beyond Italy, seeking jobs in other European countries and even in the Soviet Union and the Eastern Bloc nations. To obtain the quantity of revenue she was seeking, Danieli made the sales trips herself. The results included contracts to build a rolling mill in Sweden and to build a 750,000-ton-a-year steel mill and a bundling plant in the U.S.S.R.

Because she had the courage to make moves that no one else had dared to try, Danieli built her company into a world-class operation that now locks horns with Mitsubishi, Hitachi, NKK, and Krupp, and that also requires the courage of a lion.

The wellsprings of courage seem to generate a kind of vision that allows people to look at an insurmountable problem and see directly through it to the only right solution. At age 16, in the depths of the Great Depression, Jeno Paulucci, who was to found Chun King Corporation, worked in a grocery store in Duluth, Minnesota. One warm day, the store's refrigerator broke down, causing eighteen crates of bananas to develop brown-speckled skin. The bananas were otherwise undamaged, but because of their unusual appearance, the store owner told his young employee to take them outside and sell them at bargain prices. Jeno, however, was a man of courage and vision, even at that young age. He took the fruit outside, made a sign saying "Argentine Bananas," and began shouting about the shipment of exotic fruit. Within three hours he had sold all eighteen crates at a price four cents per pound higher than that of ordinary bananas.

In selecting your war buddies, look for the ones who understand that winning is merely getting up one time more than you have been knocked down.

AN UNDERSTANDING OF LEVERAGE The final characteristic needed by your work-out and turn-around war buddies is an appreciation for and understanding of leverage. There are three kinds of leverage—financial, communication, and time. Communication leverage is the ability to persuade people to do things for you that they had no intention of doing until you asked them to. Financial leverage is the use of borrowed money. Time leverage is getting accounts payable dates delayed and getting accounts receivable dates shortened.

Borrowing capital, of course, means going into debt, a reality with which most businesspeople are comfortable. But, as you will see, the kind and amount of financial leverage that you and your war buddies may have to incur could create personal exposure. (Fortunately, there are means of minimizing the degree of personal risk, as we will see in Stage 3: Back-to-the-Wall Street-Fight Tactics.) In order to incur mountains of financial leverage, your corps must have sufficient faith in its redirect-and-grow plan as well as the cooperation of every member.

But it is *heart* that will focus your people—the unseen glue that holds everyone together. You will see signs of it in the way your lieutenants walk—a modified swagger, coupled with speed and a quick step; in the way they talk—clear, to the point, and with the straight stuff; and in their appearance—a simple dress code with minimal accessories that exudes an ease of getting it together. This is your team, "officers and gentlemen," every one (regardless of gender), ready for any crisis no matter how large.

Now, you are in your conference room, you have written your script, and your key players are on the edge of their seats. An awkward moment overcomes the group, and there is silence.

You ask them, "Do we have the right players to pull our company through the crises we have just discussed?"

The objective here is to elicit strong commitments from your people and to convey to all present the seriousness with which you take the possibility of bad times. After the meeting, the committed players will probably want to hang around and let you know where they stand.

DEALING WITH THE EFFECTS OF A CRISIS

Your primary targets in navigating your company through a period of uncertainty are the minds of the people who might block you. Victory does not lie in crushing them, but in out-thinking them via moral and intellectual strength. You must frustrate your creditors' plans, drive wedges between competitors who form alliances against you, and make allies for your company among customers, suppliers, lenders, and investors. As Sun Tzu wrote 2,500 years ago:

> To subdue the enemy without fighting is the acme of skill.*

If a creditor seizes your bank accounts with a writ of attachment, keep an accurate record of the damages that the writ inflicts on your business. Over a period of months, measure the flow of damages caused by bounced checks and the inability to meet commitments. Then list these damages in your counter claim. At this point, your company is at war with the creditor, but you can bring the creditor to the settlement table by contacting members of the creditor's board of directors. Inform them that their directors' and officers' liability insurance—which most large corporations purchase for their directors—will not protect them if you win your damage claim because the creditor's officers acted negligently. By creating a division in the creditor's board of directors you may "subdue the enemy without fighting."

Circumnavigate your opponents, particularly the ones with financial resources greater than those your company pos-

---

* Sun Tzu, *The Art of War.*

sesses. Avoid a battle of dollars with a giant corporation that can outspend you in a legal war. File a counter claim against a bank or supplier that has legitimately damaged your company. Then, if the bank or supplier is publicly held, make certain that your damage claim is footnoted in the corporation's SEC filings. Once you have done that, you can obtain a list of the corporation's institutional stockholders and inform them that the corporation may lose several million dollars in a damage claim. Inform the financial press as well so that the small investor is notified at the same time as the institutional stockholders.

Giant, bureaucratic corporations will knuckle under to queries from the SEC and large stockholders. If their board members are concerned about personal liability for management's actions, the pressure will become unbearable, and you will receive a settlement offer. Bureaucratic corporations have three things in common: they are big, they are rich, and they are chicken-livered. You are not chicken-livered. You move swiftly and deftly, and you work smart. When the big guys move swiftly by securing writs of attachment, offsetting bank accounts, withholding shipments, or returning goods after signing firm purchase orders, they open themselves up to damage claims. That gives you your opening, and you must strike.

Like Hugh Liedtke, CEO of Pennzoil, do not think that a high and mighty organization such as Texaco can trample all over your acquisition and get away with it. The Texaco managers knew that what they were doing to Pennzoil was unethical. If not, why did they, their lawyers, and their investment bankers obtain indemnifications from the Texaco board of directors before snatching Getty Oil away from Pennzoil? In short, do not be afraid of the size of your opponent. The bigger they are, the harder they fall—especially when they run into your trip wire.

Appear weak to the big guys and strong to the little guys. Feign impoverishment and destitution to the big corporations that burn you badly. While their lawyers are writing memorandums stating that they almost have you in bankruptcy, the big guys will be receiving memorandums from their auditors, their frightened directors, their worried investors, and a watchful SEC, all questioning them about the lawsuit.

I am suggesting a scenario that will require intrepid behavior on your part. But will your war buddies respond appropriately? Will they have the heart for it? Will a confused and nervous head of marketing be able to handle calls from your industry trade journal concerning creditor lawsuits? You want the article to appear in order to show a flow of damages. He wants the article *killed* because it may damage sales.

"Sure it may damage sales. It may caution other suppliers. It may do a lot of things," you tell him. "But it may show us who our true friends really are. It may win sympathy orders. It may cause new suppliers to surface. And it may win us a big damage award."

If this marketing manager can't play rope-a-dope as Muhammad Ali did with George Foreman in Zaire—taking dozens of punches until the opponent gets weary and easy to knock out—he may not be the best man for the job. He probably lacks the heart to stand hip to hip with you through the darkest hours of battle.

Emulate the Pioneer Mother

Visualize, if you can, one of those Hollywood westerns from the 1950s. The cattle rustlers burn down the ranch, shoot the brave husband through the heart, and make off with fifty head of cattle. The posse arrives, and the sheriff strides up to the soot-blackened widow who is hugging and caressing her frightened children.

He drawls, "Looks like you'd better come back to town, ma'am. Thar ain't nothin' left of this ranch."

She sets her jaw, and with eyes so sharp they cut into your heart, she replies, "This is our land, and we're stayin' right here to defend it 'til we die."

If you can visualize the strength and determination of a pioneer mother, you are ready for the task that lies ahead.

Pioneer families were good at crisis management because they frequently emigrated from an oppressive country where they may have experienced the sudden conscription or false imprisonment of the father or the oldest son. Studies of thousands of war-torn American families have shown that war, the stressor event, is a *variable*, not a constant; the hardships that it causes can propel the family members to higher levels of strength and achievement. In studying this phenomenon, I found that 60 percent of the four hundred successful entrepreneurs I interviewed had suffered a form of serious deprivation.* These stressors included an absent father, the necessity to drop out of school and work in order to supplement the family's income, serious childhood illness, and escape from a dictatorial and oppressive foreign country.

Most families have had a long history of troubles and have worked out procedures and a division of responsibility for meeting crises as they arise. Even though the family is badly organized for problem solving, it has been doing a better job of it than any other organization you can name. Families are heavily weighted with dependents; they cannot freely reject weak members and recruit stronger ones. Its members receive unearned acceptance; they pay no price for belonging. In short, the family is an awkward decision-making group, poorly equipped to withstand stress, yet society has assigned it the heaviest responsibilities for meeting the emotional needs of all citizens, young and old.

You are the pioneer mother of your company. To prepare everyone for possible battles ahead, it is critical that you identify the issues that could lead to crisis: give the issues names and descriptions, put them on the table, measure them, touch and feel them, talk about them, and precipitate crises—dress rehearsals, if you prefer—in order to learn how to deal with them if they occur.

Give Meaning to the Stressor

The ability to ride out the stressor event without paralysis or disorganization depends on what meaning your company gives

---

* A. David Silver, *The Entrepreneurial Life* (New York: John Wiley & Sons, 1983).

Figure 2.1 *How a Stressor Event Leads to a Crisis*

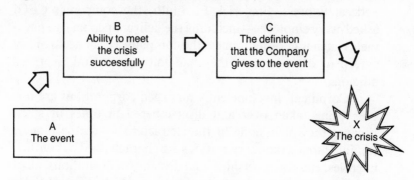

to the stressor. The conceptual framework of the stressor-to-crisis event is presented in Figure 2.1.

The second and third determinants—company resources and definitions of the event—lie within the company itself and must be seen in terms of the company's structures and values. The hardships of the event, which make up the first determinant, lie outside the company and are an attribute of the event itself.

Your company's *crisis-meeting resources* will determine the company's capacity for meeting obstacles and for steering the company away from its points of greatest vulnerability. Crisis-meeting resources include agreement by all members as to role structure, subordination of personal ambitions to the organization's goals, and satisfaction within the organization that the emotional needs of its members are being met by the goals toward which the company is collectively moving. Elegant crisis-meeting tactics begin with the manner in which telephone calls are answered and messages are taken, and they extend to the appearance of your product when it arrives at your customer's loading dock. Everyone from top to bottom must play their role during the crisis. Incompatible crisis-meeting resources must be dealt with by serious, open discussion between department heads. If one department head is unwilling to accept the organization's definition of the stressor event or the organization's plans for meeting the crisis, then he or she must be replaced in order for the company to move collectively toward meeting its goals.

In one of the more difficult moments in the early days of Federal Express, Frederick E. Smith, the company's CEO, asked every employee—including the delivery people—to pawn their watches in order to meet the company's cash needs. They agreed to do it because they had faith in Federal Express's mission.

Corpulent, incompetently managed corporations are forever being taken over and dismembered in times of stress because they have none of the characteristics of the pioneer family. Bureaucratic corporations are characterized by conflicting roles, class memberships, and diversity of aspirations, all of which create a cascade of stressors and which never nucleate into a single crisis that everyone can rally around and spill blood for. Students of the Civil War attribute the South's initial military successes (when outnumbered ten to one) to the willingness of her young men to fight and die for their way of life.

A crisis in full gallop is a highly animated calliope of lawyers demanding, collectors threatening, process servers delivering, terminated employees cajoling, customers worrying, bankers fretting, suppliers wringing their hands, and employees wondering whether they can find jobs when the hammer falls on them. There is a cacophony of noises led by the trumpeting telephones, the word processors printing like dozens of discordant pianos, the facsimile transfer machines tweeting like a band of hysterical piccolos, and people scurrying quickly from office to office with news of the latest threat, demand, suit, or shut-off notice. The CEO's office reverberates with voices over the squawk box and live voices describing the minute by minute hits that the company is taking: "Can't use the American Express card.... The bank wants the overdraft covered.... Sally Smith has brought a wrongful termination action....We are out of containers in the shipping department.... A customer is holding up an $80,000 order until it sees our latest financial statement....There's a lawyer on the telephone saying he represents two of our creditors, and he will put us into Chapter VII tomorrow morning if he doesn't get paid in full by certified check." A crisis is intense. It is like mud-wrestling with an octopus in a noisy disco.

In the brain-pounding, tension-filled days of a crisis run wild, there is no place for pink-cheeked, buttoned-down, obsequious managers, each genuflecting for promotion. There is no role for the personally ambitious, for the blame-placers, for the news-leakers, or for the nine-to-fivers.

A strong-willed pioneer mother would "slap these children up 'side the head and knock some sense into 'em." Then she would send them out of the cabin to gather wood for a camp fire, to mend the fences, or to find the cattle that were driven away. You must do the equivalent. Select the value-added players, those who sing out of the company choirbook, and show the others the door.

Adjust to the Crisis

Your company will succeed largely in terms of its members performing their roles. One major effect of crisis is to cause changes in these role patterns. You will find several managers who will volunteer to take a 30 percent cut in pay. A young lady in the secretarial pool will meekly ask you for a meeting and quickly tell you that her uncle manages a large pool of capital and that she would be willing to make an introduction for you. The accounts payable clerks may volunteer to work weekends without overtime pay. With shifting expectations, it is necessary for members of the organization to work out different patterns, and they will follow your lead if you are clear, honest, and fearless. Until the company has worked out its plan for survival, the company will have to go through a period of adjustment.

Before your company is affected by the downturn in the economy, you and your key people must establish a *script* delineating what will be said to outsiders in the event the company enters a crisis. People outside the company will hear about the problem or perhaps they will hear that a "blow has been struck" but will not know more than that. Company members must adjust to their relationships with outsiders. Who should be told? Who should not be told? Should the ones who are told be told everything? You must write a script for your employees to let them know what to say and to whom. There is a need-to-know principle that requires *role playing* by members of the organization. Those who need to know should be told: "Yes, I don't want to bore you or burden you with all the details, but you should know that we have a problem. We think we understand it, and we are dealing with it. We will come out of it very well. Just watch us."

The outsider will respond by wishing you well or perhaps by telling you that you are finally getting your just deserts. But from the response, you will be able to gauge the degree of help or comfort that this person will provide. Some outsiders will say, "Know that we're thinking about you, and if we can help, please call us. We mean that sincerely." This is the kind of friend we all need. But others will turn their backs on you until you climb out of trouble and up to a status greater than theirs. Then they will be the first to say, "See, I knew you could do it."

Sun Tzu wrote that warfare is based on deception. The skilled general creates shapes to confuse and delude the enemy. Because enemies may be competitors or creditors, you must show strength to one while feigning weakness to the other. Move intangibly, like "a ghost in the starlight;"* obscurely, silently, so that the enemy cannot determine the true strength of your numbers. Make your reports to the outside clear to your friends and confusing to your enemies.

When a crisis develops, there is a downward slump in the organization. Work is done with less enthusiasm. Conflicts within the organization are expressed or converted into tensions. Relations become strained. Eventually the company can begin to disintegrate. When the leader intercedes and begins to create order, things improve. Through trial and error as well as thoughtful planning and sacrificing, new routines are put into effect and members of the company reach new agreements about how the goals are to be reached. Much can be learned from observing the dynamics of a troubled nuclear family.

Students of alcoholic families have identified how the family can successfully adjust to their crisis, which provides us

---

* Sun Tzu, *The Art of War,* p. 41.

with a guide for our companies. The stages of adjustment closely parallel those of a company on its way to recovery:

1. Attempts to deny the problem.
2. Attempts to eliminate the problem.
3. Disorganization.
4. Attempts to reorganize in spite of the problem.
5. Efforts to escape the problem; the decision to separate from the alcoholic spouse (leave the troubled company).
6. Reorganization of the family without the spouse. (Key personnel think of starting their own company.)
7. Reorganization of the entire family, with a stronger bond than ever.

The adjustment to crisis can be shown as a roller coaster in profile. Naturally, a company cannot go through a bumpy, roller coaster ride without some personal shocks. Weaker companies lose members at the earlier stages through either shock, disbelief, numbness or mourning. Well-integrated and adaptable companies, particularly those who are well-organized before the crisis, take the roller coaster ride in stride. They are invulnerable to it, and rise to a higher level of homeostasis after the crisis is past.

A company that experiences drastic demoralization in the midst of a crisis was probably poorly organized and not well-integrated before the crisis. It habitually treated all problems by either ignoring them or over-reacting: in fact, it was crisis-prone. Many companies try to escape the problems by jaw-boning, a public relations attack, or as Itel did, by presenting false financial information to the public. An active denial system prolongs and deepens a crisis. It delays implementing the plans that could save the company. Osborne Computer Corp., the first manufacturer of portable personal computers, went out of business to the chagrin of a dozen venture capital investors because its management team did not plan ahead for crises; did no crisis forecasting and had set up no plans to mitigate the hardships of crisis. Members of the organization were self-centered and had very short-term—what we call "working for their paychecks"—goals. They thought their venture capital backers would bail them out. Alas, they were looking outside for help when the palliatives should have come from within.

The Ecological System

The company in crisis must not view itself as a lonely warrior. It is like a fallen linebacker who has other players who will help him back to his feet, and a team doctor who will tape him up and send him back into the game. Your suppliers need a good customer. Your banks need to be repaid. Your insurance agent wants to keep earning commissions. And the list goes on.

Thus when a genuine crisis exists, members of the community must be informed at some level that a problem exists, and their helpfulness must be solicited. This takes planning, because the news blurted out or leaked out improperly could send the supplier or customer or banker into a personal roller coaster ride of disbelief—numbness—mourning—despair. This reaction to the crisis could be punitive for the company, and lead it to a reaction that could sink your ship. Therefore, the members of the company's community who need to know must be told what they need to know with a great deal of forethought and preparation. Sun Tzu wrote: "Subtle and insubstantial, the expert leaves no trace; divinely mysterious, he is inaudible. Thus he is master of his enemy's fate."*

Crisis Formulation

When oil prices fell sharply in 1985, John Madden, President of Houston's Rex Machinery ($30 million sales), realized that oil drillers would have little need for drilling equipment, Rex's primary product. Madden assumed that the crisis would be deep and prolonged. What would the industry need? After careful consideration, he came up with three needs not being addressed: (1) a means of getting rid of equipment, (2) a way to obtain less expensive used equipment, and (3) a mechanism for carting away and storing equipment. Madden formed three new

* Sun Tzu, *The Art of War,* p. 97.

businesses: moving, warehousing, and used equipment sales. Then he moved middle level managers from new equipment sales to head the three new divisions. The results? Rather than stand by and watch itself slide into bankruptcy, Rex's overall sales and earnings grew as the three newly formed divisions responded splendidly to the new needs of the marketplace.

To predict and define the kind of crisis that can strike your industry—product obsolescence, industry downturn, or regional recession—begin by analyzing symptoms. Keep your ear to the ground. Routinely talk with your customers or clients to determine what they fear and what steps they might take in the short term. Do they plan to become more liquid? Do they intend to reduce inventories? Cut back from three shifts to two? Reduce their advertising budgets? Are they adopting a "bunker" mentality? In other words, is the ground vibrating with impending disaster?

As you formulate the potential crisis, create a notebook of facts. Write your own questions in the notebook: Is the crisis mentality forming among all of my customers and suppliers? Is it geographic, demographic, or psychographic? What are the trade journals reporting? Contact The Newsletter Clearinghouse in Rhinebeck, New York, to obtain names of the newsletters that deal with economic indicators, recessions, and the issues of uncertain times. Conduct your own telemarketing campaign to see how your customers and suppliers might react to a radically changing economy. Take your bankers to lunch and ask them about changes in local trends and in their banks' lending policies. In short, gather as much intelligence as you can. Not only will you be able to glean the potential problems ahead but, like John Madden, you may also be able to forecast new products and services created by the crisis itself.

Gain Time

Your most important asset in the survival game is time. In anticipation of a crisis reorganize your life so that you gain up to two more hours per day. Put a cot or sofa bed in your office, as Ted Turner did when he was working eighteen-hour days to keep Turner Broadcasting Company afloat.

Simplify your extracurricular activities. Cut off time-consuming events and certain community activities that require your participation. Have two suits and a packed bag (including toiletries and two changes of clothing) ready in your office. Learn how to steam out wrinkles in the hotel shower. Avoid jewelry and large metal key rings that set off airport security devices. Make certain your car will not need repairs for twelve to eighteen months. Purchase airline tickets in advance by cashing in your frequent flyer credits, and carry them with you to avoid waiting in line at airline counters. Keep more petty cash on hand for sudden, unexpected trips. Maintain at least one credit card well below its limit so that you can charge hotel rooms and car rentals at any time. Do the same with at least one bank debit card.

Establish new rules for your staff in order to maximize their time and efficiency. Eliminate lunches out, except when there is a cash-generating purpose. Change the parking rules to permit customers to park near your entrance. Contact the spouses of all key employees with a memorandum informing them of the need for longer hours and promising them a bonus at the end.

In the 1975-76 recession, Robert Luedke was called in to do a work-out for the seriously undercapitalized and overextended Mine & Smelter Supply Company in Denver, Colorado. At the time, the company was a $60 million (revenues) distributor of mining equipment in the Rockies. Luedke hired me as his financial consultant, and we mapped out an informal plan of reorganization that included spinning off parts of the company to generate cash and stretching the creditors until the cash could be generated. We knew that the going would be rough and that we needed to shore up the morale of the personnel. Luedke sent a letter home to the spouses of those employees whose dedication was crucial for the company's survival. The letter said simply that the company was experiencing a crisis and that Joe or Jim would have to come in early, stay late, and perhaps work on weekends. The letter promised a bonus once the work-out had been accomplished, and the envelope included a fifty-dollar bill as an expression of good faith.

The effect was immediate. The personnel developed a

cheerfulness like that seen at Little League games when the littlest player gets a hit. Before the letter, when Luedke and I walked through the accounting department, faces turned up, and twenty pairs of eyes searched our faces for signs of gloom and doom. After the letter, when we walked through the accounting department, no one looked up; they continued with business as usual, negotiating stretch-outs with suppliers or talking to customers about faster payment.

The Name Game

That wasn't all that Luedke and I did. We sold company-owned Cadillacs, cancelled club memberships, bought meals for people who worked at their desks during lunch, and gave nicknames to the crisis and its components. This latter strategy drew all personnel into the game of crisis management, or as many managers call it, the "survival game."

A medium-sized creditor who kept threatening involuntary bankruptcy was called "LeMay," after General Curtis LeMay who wanted to bomb Viet Nam off the face of the planet. Whenever our LeMay called the company with a demand for "payment or else," the chief financial officer would stick his head out of his office and yell, "Who wants to take LeMay?" At that, several payables clerks would shout back, "Let me have Ol' Bombs Away. I haven't had him in a while."

Bob Luedke had a nickname as well—a moniker that said we looked affectionately to him for leadership. He was known as the "Wheelbarrow" because someone heard me say that his balls were so big he had to walk with a wheelbarrow in front of him.

Other creditors were known as the "Whisper," the "Lisp," and the "Hammer." The Hammer was going to nail our whatevers to the wall. He was tough to deal with, so I was assigned the Hammer. My strategy was to join him in haranguing the guilty parties who had "lied" to him, trashing the innocents, and generally making him happy that, although he wasn't getting paid, we were flinging his least favorite people into the copper smelters he had sold us and melting their bodies into mush.

The Nature of a State of Crisis

Whereas stress is a negative condition, crisis has growth-promoting potential. Stress is a burden under which a person either survives or cracks. Crisis, on the other hand, is a catalyst that disturbs old habits, generates new responses, and inspires new developments. A crisis is a call to action. The challenge it provokes may bring forth new coping mechanisms that serve to strengthen the individual's adaptive capacity.*

Gerald Caplan defined crisis as an "upset in a steady state." The company strives to maintain a state of equilibrium with a series of adaptive maneuvers and problem-solving activities. Over the course of days and weeks of normal operations, many situations occur in which discontinuities disturb the equilibrium. These discontinuities are routinely dealt with through conventional adaptive mechanisms such as replacing personnel, rolling over a loan, or intensifying customer services.

However, in a state of crisis, the habitual responses are inadequate in scope and do not achieve the needed balance. Crises produce serious threats to the integrity of the company, and this creates anxiety. Losses can result in depression. Therefore, the company must mobilize energetically in order to solve whatever threatens its equilibrium.

Response to Crisis

The proper response to crisis is threefold: (1) take the impact head-on, (2) recoil from it, and (3) begin energizing solutions. When a company does not respond properly, solutions do not materialize, so the company becomes disorganized and begins to disintegrate. Here are the steps necessary for responding to a crisis effectively:

1. *Perception.* Further the correct perception of the situation by seeking new information and by keeping the problem in front of you.

---

* Lydia Rapoport, "The State of Crisis: Some Theoretical Considerations," *The Social Service Review* 27(2) (1962).

2. *Nomination.* Manage the effects on personnel by giving names to the crisis-provokers.
3. *Delegation.* Develop procedures for seeking and using help outside the company and give tasks to these outside helpers.

PERCEPTION Working your way through a crisis requires correct perception of the crisis-producing events. Sometimes it is as simple as a production layout problem causing production delays, downtime, and defective products. Other times it is a criminal indictment.

On January 31, 1975, Fred Smith, the CEO of Federal Express Corporation, was "indicted for obtaining funds from the Union Bank by the use of false documents. And, on Monday, February 3, a warrant was issued for his arrest. But this was only part of his trouble: late the same night he had been indicted, he hit and killed a pedestrian who was jaywalking."* Although Smith was removed from the company by its board of directors, the company lost $26 million and was overdue on a $49 million equipment loan. Smith was acquitted in December 1975, but his teammates had acquitted him months earlier by threatening resignation unless the board reinstated him as CEO.

Perception is based on what is known as *directed remembering.* You hear or see a particular fact, merge it into your memory bank, relate it to other experiences and then say, "Aha!"

For example, if the crisis-provoking event is in the area of cash flow, apply directed remembering to everything you know about cash, banks, wire transfers, letters of credit, selling assets, speeding collections, discounting accounts receivable, and the like. But that's not all. You need to use visualization and imagination techniques. Relate your need for cash to a tank of water. How many ways can you get water (cash) into the tank in the shortest period of time? Do you need more nozzles? Hoses? More water carriers? Go to a thesaurus and look up the "right

---

* Robert A. Sigafous, *Absolutely Positively Overnight: The Story of Federal Express* (Mentor, 1983), pp. 115-116.

word" for *fill*. You will see the nouns *padding, stuffing, filler,* and *fullness*. And you will see the verbs *load, shoal, fill up,* and *silt up*. One of these may provide you with a visual key to the correct perception of the crisis.

Sometimes perceiving is inexact. Like the artisans in Plato's cave, you are chained in place staring at shadows on the wall. You cannot see the shadow casters, but you must make *judgments* about them based on the shapes of their shadows. Once again, you rely on directed remembering. Much as the movie viewer recognizes that "the villains wear black hats," so the businessperson may interpret shadows on the wall as, "Our deficits are running too long to convince our bank to loan." Be careful not to interpret or second-guess others. Perceptions get distorted under pressure.

NOMINATION   We discussed the "name game" earlier; now, extend it. Give names or assign symbols to the crisis-provoking events—make them momentous, memorable, important. For example, buy small statues of Greek wrestlers at war and put them on the desks of your controllers and salespersons. Label the first, "Charles (your controller) Battling Jim (the company's banker)." And label your salesman's figurine, "Bill Chokes an Order from Valued Customer."

Put an appropriate *Peanuts* cartoon on your production manager's bulletin board, perhaps showing Snoopy's gritty management of the little birds that interfere with his daily regimen. In doing this, you are discharging tension. This is a first step to mastering the problem.

For the person you assign to lay off one hundred people in administration, label a stuffed rhinoceros "Mike the Merciless" and put it in his office. You are saying, "I know I stuck you with a bad job, and you are a soft-hearted guy who did a tough job well. Way to go."

Give nicknames to your enemies. Call your toughest bill collector the most ridiculous word you can think of, like "Al the Anteater" or "Godzilla Gorilla," or better yet, have your accounts payable clerks choose terms of endearment, with the winning nomination receiving a fifty-dollar prize. Sounds ridiculous? Believe me, you can make a terrific impact on morale by using the name game. Humor is a superb morale booster, and you can make the crisis seem both real and manageable by using it pointedly.

DELEGATION   Michael Dingman, 56, chief executive officer of Henley Group, is known to his many fans on Wall Street as a "Class-A Schmoozer." Dingman knows how to work through his managers: he delegates everything, then strokes his managers by laying on the charisma. Their ability to get the job done is enhanced by what Felix G. Rohatyn of Lazard Freres & Company calls "schmoozing." This literally means sitting with people, talking to them, laying it on thick, and charming the pants off them. It breeds loyalty, and if it is genuine friendliness, it works.

Do not delegate without staying in touch. Keep close tabs on and demonstrate your concern for the task you have delegated. You are dealing with many personalities. You may have a personality tailor-made for crisis, but your teammates may need extra reassurance.

When you delegate to people outside the organization, visit them frequently. If an outsider is assigned the task of selling your headquarters building and leasing it back, stay on top of him. Take him to dinner and review his progress. Go over the details again and again. Then schmooze him with your compliments. Talk him into believing that this sale-leaseback is the heart of your survival strategy. Help him raise his self-esteem. Ask him to report on the progress of his mission every day. Give him your private telephone number or home number. Encourage his speed. Let him know that an entire company, perhaps a whole region, turns its anxious eyes to him. It will work.

Crises Have Time Limits

Do facing desperation and riding through it safely prepare you and your managers for future crises? The answer is a resounding "Yes!" I believe that it is of greater benefit to a company's key players than steady growth. Why? Because we learn the most important fact about crises: they have time limits. Crises do not go on forever. The better prepared and more adaptive the company before the crisis, the shorter the period of reorganization. Moreover, regardless of the reasons for the crisis, the company that weathers it becomes so lean and efficient that it is poised for immediate growth once the crisis is over.

Crises instruct us that we must organize our company so that we are not dismembered by them. We must develop an action-oriented code of behavior like marines who hit the beach and fire in all directions.

Communication During Crises

Your responses to information are of critical importance to survival; lines of communication must be open to you around the clock. To clarify what should or should not be communicated, you must continually explain the company's mission to your key personnel, and you must explain how you expect them to deal with events and data. Clearly define the differences between stressor events (problems that may occur) and true crises (real and potentially devastating events). Moreover, your ideas about what constitutes an appropriate response to one or the other should match theirs. Key personnel will perceive stressor events as crises unless they are told otherwise— especially those people who have recently worked for behemoth organizations and whose reaction to problems is to make them worse through active denial, through massive litigation, or through a public relations blast that obfuscates reality beyond anyone's ability to separate truth from fiction.

Hicks Waldron, chief executive officer of Avon Products, apparently lost sight of what was happening at Avon's Foster Medical subsidiary in 1986. Foster management failed to foresee and prepare for a change in the government's reimbursement recertification guidelines for Foster's oxygen therapy service (a $100-million-per-year source of revenues). The government had refused to pay Foster for the oxygen services it had rendered to Medicare patients, and alas, Foster had to give its service away. Obviously, someone failed to communicate.*

Communications are a critical requirement during hard times. Communication is the means for carrying messages, feelings, and ideas to the various members of the company (internal communication) and to the outside community (external communication). You must decide which messages are worth transmitting, and this will be influenced by the value system that you have created within your company. Let all communications, internal and external, reflect the company's value system. This requires paying close attention to details.

Paying Attention to Details

People get sloppy when things are going well. But when there is a full-scale, company-threatening crisis at hand, *everyone* must pay close attention to details.

Prevent any proposal, bid, offering circular, or important letter from leaving the company unless it is completely accurate and as attractive as it can possibly be. When sending documents by courier, record the airbill number. When asking that a check be sent via overnight courier, give the check sender your account number, or better yet, send him a courier envelope and your self-addressed airbill. If you have convinced the customer to wire transfer funds, be sure to add the receiving bank's *routing* number. Then alert your bank that a wire transfer is coming, and ask to be called when it arrives.

In the midst of a crisis, the office may become chaotic. Papers can get lost; the janitorial service may throw away papers that are inadvertently placed on the floor. Strive for neatness. After all, a worried supplier or banker may drop in unexpectedly, and suspecting chaos, he will look for it. Do not let the tough times translate into sloppiness. Be particularly careful that everyone is paying close attention to details. Remember Mies van der Rohe's dictum: "God is in the details."

---

* *Forbes* (January 2, 1987), p. 84.

Crisis As a Turn-On

Keep the reasoning simple yet elegant. Absorb data like a sponge, but relate it to simple facts, such as volleyball games or key words. Relieve tension with nicknames. They make the crisis seem manageable. Delegate with stroking. Permit the crisis to turn you on. Let it turn your managers on as well. When they hear footsteps and see a crisis around every corner, encourage them to develop a downside plan that will be ready to be put into effect when the upside plan fails. Help everyone develop instinctive adaptive capabilities.

Crises have their lighter sides. A client of my firm was being visited by the sheriff so frequently that a friendship developed, and my client helped the sheriff start a security guard business.

Crises pull us together because we close ranks for protection. Personnel become better friends. Everyone strives to tell a better gallows joke to cut the tension.

In the midst of a crisis, even the smallest victory becomes a major event. Collecting $1,200 from a 120-day account you had written off becomes a major event. The cash came from heaven, so share the good fortune with the men and women in the trenches. Buy lunch for everyone, or give everyone a crisp fifty-dollar bill. It will turn everyone on, and the light at the end of the tunnel may seem brighter.

SUMMARY

The better your company is organized before a crisis, the higher it will springboard out of the crisis. When your company is entering nervous times, gather your division heads into the conference room and encourage them to voice their fears and frustrations. Anyone who denies that the stressors could lead to a crisis is probably not going to be ready to help you pull through the crisis when it hits. The inevitable period of self-pity and denial must be gotten through quickly.

Then you can deal with the crisis. First, become fearless and determined. As commander, select your war buddies on the criteria of their heart, courage, loyalty, and ability to cooperate. Gather and perceive information quickly. Give facts their most simple meaning. Give the crisis-provokers nicknames. Relieve tensions and unify your corps by encouraging them to attack these names. Delegate missions, particularly with outsiders, and honor your soldiers. Begin to pull the outside helpers into the problem and use their resources. Create internal and external channels of communications that project what you want projected and when. Finally, pay careful attention to details.

Once you have done these things, your company is prepared for a crisis. It is organized. Everyone knows the plan of attack. The crisis-provokers have names; they are real. The crisis-deniers have been terminated. The stressors have been identified and labeled, and you can deal with them openly and effectively.

CREATING GENUINE LIQUIDITY

Chapter Three

Sell Something

In the long, hot summer of 1976 I spent many afternoons negotiating with Charles Tandy, founder of Tandy Corporation and owner of the Radio Shack chain. The country was in the pit of a recession, and Tandy was trying to sell several businesses in order to invest the cash in Radio Shack's TRS-80 microcomputer. My firm was trying to acquire Allied Electronics Corporation, an electronics wholesaler, from Tandy via a leveraged buy-out (LBO)—the acquisition of a company by borrowing the purchase price with loans secured by the target company's assets and then selling off parts of the target company or generating a cash flow from the target company to repay the loans. Tandy, who had bought and sold many businesses, was teaching me a thing or two about genuine liquidity.

I would fly into Fort Worth and drive to Tandy's office in the downtown area (where he would be holding court with some "good ol' boys" from East Texas), and Tandy would usually greet me with an offhand welcome such as, "Hope you've got something good to offer me, son, because I'm busier than a one-legged ass kicker." Whenever I proposed a new price or new terms, Tandy always declined with some funny line that would set his buddies to howling with laughter—"If you set the price, then I'll set the terms, but you can't have the cow and the milk both." Tandy knew more about how to squeeze cash out of assets than any person I had ever met, and he did not want to take back any notes, or "paper" as he called them. One offer in particular had him taking back more paper than cash. Tandy rocked back in his chair, roared with laughter, and then spouted a string of the funniest, dirtiest expressions I have ever heard, his way of explaining that he wanted to cash out of Allied Electronics. He turned down one of my noncash proposals with, "That offer is like a fart, son. It's not ready." And so it went. (I was not clever enough to think of borrowing on Allied Electronics' customer list to raise the cash that Tandy was holding out for. Some other buyer did just that, and he is the richer for it.)

Tandy grew up dirt poor in the dust-bowl depression of East Texas, and he knew the difference between cash and any facsimile thereof. He knew in the depths of his soul that cash is king, that there is no substitute, and that he would not trade a business that generated cash flow for anything other than an all-cash purchase price. He created an indelible image in my mind of what it is like to live in a world without cash, and the lesson was not lost on me.

With the sale of Allied, Pier 1, and Tandy Crafts, Tandy generated the cash to enter the personal computer business, and although he did not live to see it, Tandy Corporation has become a significant player in the $9 billion (1987 revenues) personal computer business. The lesson: if you are going to springboard out of a crisis, you had better raise cash.

A WORLD WITHOUT CASH

Think for a moment what it might be like to operate your business in a world without cash. This is the horror of horrors, the lowest point on the downside, every businessperson's worst nightmare. It is possible that if a large number of investment and commercial banks collapse, cash will vanish from the economy: purchasers will hoard cash, suppliers will ship only on COD terms, banks will shut down by the hundreds, and the

FDIC will be too broke to bail them out. The economy could gasp and wheeze for several months without cash. What do you do to survive this scenario? You get busy today—as busy as a one-legged ass kicker—and you generate cash. Make this your goal, beginning today, because soon we could be living in a world without cash.

You don't believe it? Reread some history books on the Great Depression. Read about the Irish potato famine of 1836-1840; Ireland had no cash for nearly five years. Read about the South during the Civil War or about Japan following World War II. You will learn how people trade, barter, exchange, and invent new means of survival in order to exist in a world without cash.

Many of you cannot conceive of a severely depressed and intensely illiquid economy in which all the world is for sale but buyers are nonexistent. It could happen, and in this chapter, I discuss as many strategies as I can think of to help you create genuine liquidity.

As a first step, take a personal inventory of your company's assets and sell everything that is not needed in the business. Then consider the following cash-generating schemes, of which some may be more appropriate for distribution businesses and others may be more fitting for retailers or manufacturers.

A SUMMARY OF CASH-GENERATING SCHEMES

Maximizing credit
Bartering
Shifting costs to customers
Schlepping
Licensing
Finding off-balance sheet assets
Selling and leasing back
Adding new products to current distribution channels
Creating new income sources from established products
Using 900 numbers and one-call polling
Using direct-mail marketing
Using video logs
Using joint ventures
Using shared mail marketing
Using cable TV marketing

Franchising
Using database marketing
Learning about user groups
Brainstorming crazy ideas to get you thinking

TAKING PERSONAL INVENTORY

When you are slammed against the wall by a severe cash crisis, you know from the previous chapters on psychological adjustments to crises not to dwell on martyrdom too long. You must pass quickly through the stages of denial, anger, and blame. Forget that you are in the such-and-such business; you are not in it anymore. You are in the survival business, and you must take an inventory of the things you can sell to generate cash. There are no sacred cows in your company. Raising cash is your mission.

Here are some tips for amassing cash quickly. Examine your company's physical needs. Can you operate in a smaller space? Do you need all of your offices? All of your warehouse space? Why not rent out some offices and warehouse space to small companies? When hospital occupancy rates fell in the early 1980s, unoccupied rooms were rented out to ice cream vendors, among others, who sold their products to patients and visitors. Find several compatible companies who will pay you rent in consideraton for office space, a receptionist, a conference room, or warehouse or production space.

Intexx Corporation in Reno, Nevada, is the nation's largest manufacturer of outdoor toilets for parks, golf courses, and recreational areas, and it was growing at a rapid rate until 1986 when it suddenly lost a large General Services Administration contract that represented over half its sales. Charles E. Kaufman III, Intexx's president, sold the company's manufacturing facilities, which shrunk its gross profit margin but, at the same time, removed over $1 million of debt from its balance sheet. The decision freed up about one-fourth of Intexx's office space, so Kaufman rented the space at a profit to an engineering firm. Now, when Intexx needs engineering services, they are only a few footsteps away. The additional income helped the company's cash flow while rebuilding its revenue base.

Take a hard look at your company's inventory. If it is turning six times a year, can it possibly turn eight times a year? Ten times? Twelve times? Sure it can.

If your company is a manufacturer, ask your customers to purchase the raw materials they need and deliver them to you. You will save cash and dramatically increase inventory turns. Shadyside Stamping Corporation of Ohio produces hoods and door panels for automobile and truck manufacturers, and several customers, including Navistar, purchase the sheet steel and deliver it to Shadyside.

Do you carry finished goods inventory from one season to the next? That is cash-intensive as well. Peter B. Hollis, 44, the new CEO of Ames Department Stores, put an end to recycling seasonal inventory. Clearance sales meant that *all* unsold inventory must go at the end of each season so that nothing would be carried for twelve months.

Your company has probably accumulated extra desks, chairs, lamps, calculators, computers, file cabinets, rugs, vases, coat racks, containers, and other relics from your tycoon era. Turn them over to the junk man for cash.

Your machinery and equipment are probably being used less than full-time. Offer contract manufacturing services to other manufacturers in your region or community. Instead of one shift per day, run two shifts per day, and offer contract manufacturing on the free days. If you make a product for the domestic market, offer contract manufacturing services to foreign companies, and offer other services as well: advertising, market research, sales, customer service, and accounting.

If you own and operate vans and trucks, get into the moving business and let your rolling stock work all the time by moving other folks' goods. If this cannot happen for you, then sell the vans and trucks for cash, and hire the moving services of an independent carrier.

A pizza delivery company in Albuquerque, New Mexico, recently got into the home video business in order to increase its revenues per driver-trip. The company began a new service:

stocking home videos on consignment and offering one free video rental, or two for $1, with each pizza over $5. The drivers picked up the videos on their trips the following day. The joint businesses are doing so well, the company may begin selling and delivering rapid turnover food products to save people a trip to the store.

If someone in your firm becomes proficient at selling off used equipment, ask him or her to find out whether there is an opportunity to broker used equipment for other companies. You may identify a small but meaningful profit center. Fred Herdlick, president of Electro-Rep, a battery distributor in St. Louis, Missouri, found a niche in cleaning and restoring used batteries for utility companies and forklift operators.

Then there are people; in a scaled-down business, fewer people are needed. You can always get along with one or two fewer accounting clerks or administrative personnel. Three sales persons can share one secretary. The accounts payable department can get by with fewer bodies if you reduce your purchases of raw materials.

MAXIMIZING CREDIT

If your company is carrying accounts receivable without a receivables line of credit, contact a commercial finance company and arrange credit. For accounts receivable from corporate customers, you can borrow up to 85 percent of the invoice when you generate the sale. For existing accounts receivable, you can raise 85 percent on amounts less than ninety days old. If your accounts receivable are from individuals or governments, you might not be able to borrow on them at all unless you can document a historical record of consistently good collections. In any event, the advance rate on these less desirable accounts will be less than 80-85 percent. There are insurance companies that will guarantee the collectability of most accounts receivable for a fee. This is important if you have noncorporate or foreign accounts.

Factoring is a more expensive means of generating cash from your company's accounts receivable. Rather than loaning against accounts receivable, a factor buys them and, in so doing, assumes the collection risk. The price of factoring can be discounted as much as 16 percent per invoice, although it is typically 10-12 percent, and the customer sends payments to the factor rather than to you.

If you establish a line of credit with a commercial finance company for your accounts receivable, ask the lender whether it would be willing to provide credit against your inventory. Finished goods and raw material inventories are considered acceptable credit. The advance rates are rarely higher than 60 percent and can be as low as 30 percent. Commercial finance companies will calculate the liquidation value of your inventory—that is, the price it will bring at auction, or "under the hammer," as they call it—and advance you cash at a discount from that value. However, if the advance rate is 35 percent, for every dollar of acceptable inventory on hand, you can raise 35 cents, and the same applies to purchases. Then, as you sell the finished goods, your invoice is submitted to the factor or commercial finance company, and you receive 80-85 percent of the sales price, repay the 35 percent advance, and end up with cash in your pocket.

If your company has on its books machinery or equipment that is debt-free, you can raise cash by borrowing long-term loans against them or by selling it to an equipment-leasing company and leasing them back. The advance rate is typically 60-75 percent of the liquidation value of the asset. More on the details of this later. The same applies to your buildings or property.

Further, in most states, there are funds available from state agencies for job-saving or job-creating loans. These loans range from $10,000 to $20,000 in cash for every job your company projects it will save or create over the next two to three years. Collateral for the loans is generally the equity remaining in the company's assets after they have been pledged to conventional lenders. The interest rates on state loans are generally in the range of 6-8 percent per annum, and the term is ten to fifteen years—substantially longer than conventional loans. You have to make a "but for" case to state lenders; that is, you must convince them that but for their loan, your company would lay off fifty people or be unable to create fifty new jobs in three years.

If your company's balance sheet appears close to the one in Table 3.1, notice the amount of cash you can wring out of it via conventional and state loans.

Table 3.1 *Cash Availability from Conventional Lenders[a]*

Asset	Book Value	Acceptable or Liquidation Value	Times	Advance Rate	Equals	Initial Drawdown of the Loan
Accounts receivable	$1,000	$900	×	.80	=	$ 720
Inventory	800	600	×	.50	=	300
Equipment	$1,200	750	×	.75	=	565
Plant	300	750	×	.75	=	5,650
Total	$3,300					$2,150

[a]Amounts in thousands of dollars.

The balance sheet in Table 3.1 will generate $2,150,000 in immediate cash. But you have left some money on the table if you have not approached the economic development director in your county. Let's look at the availability for a long-term state loan at an interest rate below market. (See Table 3.2.)

Table 3.2 *Cash Availability from State Loans[a]*

Asset	Acceptable or Liquidation Value	Times	Inverse of Advance Rate	Equals	Additional Loan Value
Accounts receivable	$ 900	×	.20	=	$180
Inventory	600	×	.50	=	300
Equipment	750	×	.25	=	187
Plant	750	×	.25	=	187
Total	$3,000				$854

[a]Amounts in thousands of dollars.

In order to justify the additional $850,000, your redirect-and-grow plan must show that you can save or create at least eighty-five jobs over three years. Some states—primarily those in the sunny, tourist-welcoming Southeast and Southwest—do not provide these "but for" term loans.

Needless to say, your cash flow statements and projections must be able to demonstrate an ability to service the interest and principal repayments of the debt. To service a $3 million debt at an average interest rate of 9 percent per annum in "normal" times, you must generate earnings before interest and taxes (EBIT) of $270,000 per annum, plus at least twice that amount to repay a portion of the term loan each year, plus interest. Remember to add back noncash expenditures such as depreciation and amortization when calculating your ability to service debt.

If you need an annual EBIT of $540,000 to service $3 million in indebtedness, you can figure on needing 50 percent more in troubled times if your borrowings are tied to the prime interest rate. If they are, and if your cost of money doubles to 18 percent per annum, you will need over $800,000 per annum to service the debt.

In negotiating new loans when at the end of the diving board of what you consider a stormy economic crisis, try to put a ceiling on the interest rate if it is tied to prime, try to avoid personal guarantees, and try to include in the loan agreement a "cure period" of as much as ninety days in which to correct a default. The first two points may seem obvious as to their intent. The third point is to allow you three months to turn your company around in the event that you default on the loan and a sheriff is at the door.

There is a question of how greedy one should be at the loan window prior to a serious recession. If you are raising equity capital, there is no upper limit to how many chestnuts you should gather to keep the family fed during the long, cold winter. But loans must be repaid, and if you are unable to do so, the lender will modify your behavior.

Xicor, a semiconductor manufacturer in Milpitas, California, ended calendar year 1987 with more than $45 million in cash. However, in March 1988, it raised approximately $20 million in equity from the public for a reserve. Raphael Klein, Xicor's CEO, was asked by his underwriters why he wanted more cash, and he replied that he vividly remembered the severe recession in the semiconductor industry in 1983-84 and that he did not ever want to be caught short again.

But you cannot treat debt like equity. When borrowing money to avoid being caught short, you must do some downside planning in order to be ready to pursue several alternative plans for generating cash flow if your sales turn sour and your EBIT falls below debt service.

If your company is carrying a comfortable debt load prior to a recession, try to restructure your loans now in order to fix the interest rate on the bulk of the loans. You can do this via private placements with insurance companies or pension funds or via the sale of debentures to the public.

BARTERING

Virtually anyone can enter the barter economy and trade excess inventory for cost-saving services such as advertising space, airplane seats, hotel rooms, rental cars for company salesmen, and more. I asked Fred Tartar, founder of Deerfield Corporation, the world's leading barter company, to explain to me how Deerfield operates.

> Let's say St. Tropez Cosmetics calls me and says they would like to unload ten thousand gross of lipsticks, twelve to a box—that's about fifteen million tubes of lipstick—which is in St. Tropez's inventory for $7.5 million. Let's say I can find a home for the lipstick with various Latin American health and beauty aid distributors for $2.5 million, which is fine with St. Tropez, but the Latin Americans don't have $2.5 million in cash. "What do they have to trade?" I ask them. They tell me they have various things to trade—airline seats, prepaid rental car vouchers, and some credits from their government. The package is a little cumbersome, but I give some currencies to my client, which it converts into dollars, then I go to work on airline seats and car rental credits. I find that Hertz likes to buy the back

page of inflight magazines. So, here I am with a bunch of car rental chits which I barter with magazines to generate ads for Hertz, for which it pays the difference. Then I sell the airline seats to buyers of discount tickets for cash, and I pay my client.

I nodded politely to Tartar—I suppose everyone nods politely to him in the hopes that he will not test them on what he has just said. In any event, barter experts are creative cash generators. You can unload salable inventory on them for cash or barter chits, and through myriad peregrinations, they will move the goods to distributors who need them. The barter companies do not generate top dollar. They are a port in the storm, an island of safety in a tossing sea, a form of bail-out insurance for the company drowning in illiquid assets.

If your company is in a service industry and does not have excess inventories to barter, take stock of your underutilized service capabilities and barter them for products or services that can be converted into cash. Can your finely tuned receivables collection department provide similar services for customers in consideration for their paying you upfront or for their ordering more of your services? Do you have more printing, telephone, or computer capacity than you need? Radio and television stations frequently barter unused advertising time (or the time created due to last-minute cancellations) to brokers who resell it at discount prices to large and frequent advertisers. The tartar-cleaning toothpaste Topol is advertised almost exclusively in the space of cancelled time slots.

As you comb your inventory of barterable products and services, remember that your weaknesses may be someone else's strengths; your excesses, someone else's weaknesses. The economic community runs smoothly most of the time because of its elegant mechanism for fitting needs with suppliers.

SHIFTING COSTS TO CUSTOMERS

Ask yourself what tasks your customers can perform for themselves (without your losing any revenues) that you are presently providing for them—and, indeed, tying up cash to do so. Can you trade some of these services to the customer and free up assets or people?

There was a time when U.S. zoos and wild animal parks were exclusively public enterprises. But in the mid-1970s, Lion Country Safari discovered a means of operating such facilities with a small initial capital investment and on a profitable basis. It shifted the burden of paying for cages and energy costs to the customer. Visitors to Lion Country's wild animal parks paid for the cages (their cars) and energy costs (gasoline), as well as paying admission fees; whereas the company paid for leasing the land, paid for the animals—which, happily, reproduced— and paid for the animals' feed. A clever trade-off. The customer gained convenience and the pleasure of seeing the animals in wild habitats. Lion Country conserved cash and generated a profit by leveraging the customer's needs.

SCHLEPPING

Schlepper is Yiddish for a person with a couple of old shopping bags full of odds and ends he has picked up somewhere and intends to sell somewhere else.

In the black community, the schlepper was the "rags 'n old iron" man who pushed a cart full of odd bits down the alleys behind the houses and who would sell junk, buy junk, or swap junk as he went along shouting out his song, "Rags 'n old iron! Oh, rags 'n old iron!"

The modern version of the schlepper and the rags-n-old-iron man is the consumer products catalog or direct-mail merchandiser who sells discontinued or overstocked items. The best known entities in the consumer electronics industry are JS&A (for Joe Sugarman & Associates) and DAK (for Dean A. Kaplan). They buy unique products (whose manufacturers lack advertising and marketing dollars) from cash-constrained small manufacturers at distressed prices. Then they advertise these products in their direct-response ads or in their catalogs at prices of 25-30 percent below retail list. The strapped manufacturer can raise $10 per unit in immediate cash for a product that it would normally sell for $50.

I visited a manufacturer of one of the best-known business-software products late in 1987—fifty thousand units sold at $100 per unit. The company had recently introduced an upgrade for $400 per unit with over thirty additional features. The company was going to launch the upgraded version with a big advertising campaign, and the capital was to be raised via a new issue of its common stock. Then came Black Monday. In two months, the company's sales had fallen from $350,000 to $15,000 per month. It had no user group, and it did not have its customer names in list-rentable form. I devised an informal reorganization plan for the company and, to raise emergency cash to cover payroll and the telephone bill, we sold nine thousand boxes of the original product to software schleppers for $10 per box. The $90,000 came in the nick of time, permitting us to initiate the informal reorganization plan instead of being forced into Chapter VII and certain liquidation.

A number of the country's most successful business people began in the pawn shop and schlepper trade. Rose Blumkin, the 92-year-old founder of Nebraska Furniture Mart, which was acquired in 1986 for $90 million, came to the United States from Russia as a little girl and later helped her husband run a pawn shop until his death. With no cash and with children to feed and clothe, Rose began selling her own furniture out of her house. With her first cash receipts, she bought more used furniture, restored it and resold it. The decent way she treated the people who bought her used furniture led to customer allegiance and to her formation of the largest furniture store under one roof. Rose's motto: "Pay cash, give good quality, and never cheat nobody."

Do you know the schlepper companies in your industry? If not, scour the classified sections of your trade journals. Schleppers don't pay much for advertising, so check the small print.

LICENSING

With a full-court press on to raise cash, now is as good a time as any to license one of your products to a large corporation that services a market you do not presently address. If you manufacture industrial equipment, you might license its medical appli-cations to a distributor for that market. If you are concentrating on North America, you might license to Europe or the Far East. Some fine companies have gone this route to raise badly needed cash. Did you ever hear of Rank Xerox? The once illiquid Haloid Company, predecessor of Xerox Corpora-tion, sold the right to market in the United Kingdom and Commonwealth countries to the Rank Organization.

It is common practice among computer software compan-ies to license their products in two markets simultaneously while maintaining several plums for themselves. Licensing opportu-nities can be found among original equipment manufacturers (OEMs), such as computer manufacturers whose machines are enhanced by particular software. The OEM seeks the right to market the software to the users of its equipment, and it pays upfront either on a per sale basis, or on a royalty basis. This is known as a *horizontal market license* because the OEM sells to many end-users in various industries. For example, the word-processing software package WordStar is sold horizontally to practically every industry.

A *vertical market license* is the sale of the exclusive market-ing rights for a product to a company that can resell it only within a certain industry. Cipherlink Corporation, a software developer, licensed Coopers & Lybrand the exclusive rights to use and resell Cipherlink's "Automated Auditor" package to the accounting industry. If your product is generic, you can license several vertical market applications. Enabling Technolo-gies, a Chicago software developer, has licensed its solids-modeling software to the medical industry *and* to the printing industry. Thus, it has sold OEM licenses to computer manufac-turers that incorporate the price of Enabling's software into the price of their hardware, but only in those two industries.

A third form of license is the *territorial marketing license*, in which you sell the exclusive rights to market your product in another part of the world—a region or country you cannot reach because you cannot afford to create a sales and service organization there. United States manufacturers of medical diagnostic equipment frequently sell territorial marketing licenses because Europe and the Far East are large territories and because foreign manufacturers of health-care equipment have sales forces in place and are seeking innovative new products to sell through their established pipelines. Bear in mind that it is costly to audit the books and records of foreign licenses. Therefore, you should insist on a payment upfront, representing at least 50 percent of the first year's estimated aggregate royalty, with the next 50 percent payable in six months. If the licensee questions you on this point, tell him that you simply cannot afford to audit him at this time, nor can you afford to sue him if he shortchanges you. Thus, for the first year, you will take one-half upfront. For example, if it has been agreed that the licensee must sell a minimum of ten thousand units in the first year, if the licensee's selling price is $500, and if the royalty fee is 5 percent of the first ten thousand units, then the licensee is obligated to you for at least $250,000. It is your prerogative to demand $125,000 in cash upfront when the agreement is signed. Be sure that the licensee guarantees the second payment and that its guarantee is worth something. If the licensee has a net worth less than the guarantee, you have not been given anything of value. After all, you will want to discount the second payment with a factor or an asset-based lender and thus raise another $100,000 upfront.

Precisely define the minimum annual sales and the territory encompassed by the license. Also, put an outside date on it—say, five years—with renewal by mutual consent. You may want to regain the market that you gave up in a moment of weakness. The licensee will probably want to keep it because he paid for its development. Thus, when it comes time to renew the license, there is a strong possibility that you can raise the ante or sell the territory outright for a large fee. For ideas on shrewd territorial license deals, look no further than the Coca-Cola Bottling Companies. In 1899 the rights to sell Coca-Cola in bottles were sold to two Chattanooga lawyers by Asa Candler, who had purchased the rights to Coca-Cola from its inventor for $1,200. Although bottlers ordered the syrup from Coca-Cola, the Tennesseans created one of the great family fortunes in the South by licensing the bottling rights throughout the country.

To obtain a panoply of licensing candidates, gather the

names of the corporate planning officers of the largest corporations in the United States and in major foreign countries—most of the foreign corporations have New York or California offices. Focus on corporations that would be most likely to have a need for or a desire to resell your product. The major business magazines frequently publish lists of these large corporations, and you can telephone them for copies of their annual reports. For fastest access, order 10-K reports filed with the SEC from Disclosure, Incorporated, P.O. Box 75090, Baltimore, Maryland 21275 (800-638-8241), which sells reprints of 10-Ks and sends them out via overnight courier. In addition, many corporate planning officers belong to the Association of Corporate Growth, and it is possible to obtain a membership list by contacting them in New York City.

FINDING OFF-BALANCE SHEET ASSETS

A customer list, once appraised by a list broker, represents excellent collateral. A customer's name, if rented twenty times per year at 5 cents per name, is worth $1; 100,000 names are worth $100,000 at market value and $80,000 in loan value. If you do not have 100,000 names, pool your names with those of others in your community, and together contact a list broker.

Begin generating a customer list immediately. If your business does not lend itself to obtaining the names of its customers, devise other means of building a list of their names and addresses. If you operate cash-only restaurants, have your customers fill in their names and addresses to win a prize or to answer a questionnaire. The prize idea is the best, because it will generate more names. If you sell a product for cash, put a warranty card in the box; your customers will be delighted to tell you who they are and where they live. These names are much sought after by direct-mail marketing firms who are constantly seeking more responsive lists. In fact, if your customer list includes telephone numbers, it could be worth more than $1 per name to a list broker.

Technical know-how is also an off-balance sheet asset. A computer software company does not carry the cost on its balance sheet of developing source codes, but the company owns them. A lender might see the source code or the company's "knowledge" as lendable collateral. In the same manner, purchase orders are not assets, but they represent collateral for certain asset-based lenders.

Your company's plant and equipment may be fully depreciated and thus reflect a low value on the balance sheet. Have them reappraised to see whether there is additional collateral in the bricks and steel.

If you lease retail space, you can assign your leases to a lender in order to generate cash. Manufacturers of consumer electronics products can rent out the lists of their warranty cardholders. Or, if your logo is well known, it might be licensable to a clothing manufacturer—just as McDonald's Corporation recently did with Sears to create the McKids line of children's clothing. Thar's gold in them thar "off-balance sheet" hills.

SELLING AND LEASING BACK

Many cash-starved companies sell their plant and equipment to leasing companies in order to generate badly needed dollars. The leasing companies generally advance 75 to 85 percent of the liquidation value of the equipment and 60 to 75 percent of the market value of the plant, and the company repays the leasing company over five to seven years on the equipment lease and over seven to ten years on the building lease. Many large commercial banks and commercial finance companies have equipment-leasing divisions. To obtain financing, you will require up-to-date appraisals, audited financial statements, precisely documented statements of cash flow projections, and a sound, overall business plan. However, if your company tumbles into Chapter XI, the leasing company has title to the assets you sold it, and these assets are not available for other lenders to attach. Because of their preferred position in bankruptcy, equipment-leasing companies will expose themselves to more risks than will conventional lenders.

ADDING NEW PRODUCTS TO CURRENT DISTRIBUTION CHANNELS

Many of the heaviest upfront cash-producing marketing strategies result from some businesspeople desperately seeking a method of generating cash before the product is delivered. You may be selling a single product, such as a desktop computer, and picking up one check per sale. If so, you are foregoing the sale of software, peripherals, and service contracts—three more sales through the same channel. If you are not multiplying your sales, you are leaving money on the table.

Book publishers have a knack for pushing additional products through their primary book-distribution channels. St. Martin's Press and Simon & Schuster have many "feet on the street" calling on bookstore chains. It costs them very little to add to their lists quality books published by smaller firms, and they generate additional revenues from their sales forces.

Hard times are the best times to put some innovative products into your sales force's briefcases, into your direct-marketing catalog, or into your videolog. Originally a catalog marketer of specialized consumer electronics products, Richard Thalheimer launched *The Sharper Image* on a simple idea: inventors of digital calorie counters and automobile-seat warmers lacked the capital to market their products. Thalheimer charged them an advertising fee to show their products in *The Sharper Image* catalog, and he charged a minimum 30-percent commission on sales generated through the catalog. In time, *The Sharper Image* had sufficient profits for a public offering, and Thalheimer used the proceeds to create a new marketing channel—retail showrooms.

CREATING NEW INCOME SOURCES FROM ESTABLISHED PRODUCTS

T. George Harris, the publisher of *American Health* magazine, can point to dozens of creative income sources from a single product. In addition to sales of the magazine itself, *American Health* generates cash in many other ways:

1. Advertisements
2. Subscriber list rentals
3. Sales of "health and fitness" features to domestic newspapers
4. Sales of articles to foreign newspapers
5. Sales of audio cassettes based on a series of articles
6. Sales of video cassettes based on a series of articles
7. Sales of books based on a series of articles
8. Product endorsement fees
9. Sales of T-shirts, sweat shirts, and tote bags bearing the magazine's logo
10. Sales of related products such as dictionaries of health and fitness terms.

When I launched my investment banking firm in 1970, it immediately occurred to me that I had to generate additional sources of income to fill the cash flow valleys. Further, I perceived that many of the clients seeking my services had no idea that I existed or how to find me. I discovered that there were secondary channels for my expertise—publishing and speaking. And, in addition to the income generated, those who read my books and attended my seminars could contact me in the future to hire the services of my firm.

Other businesses similar to mine have carried the publishing-speaking channel to a higher level of sophistication. Howard Ruff, an investment counselor, offers week-long retreats for several thousand dollars per attendee. Joseph Mancuso founded the Chief Executive Officers Club and the Center for Entrepreneurial Management, which provide forums across the country for selling Mancuso's books, tapes, and newsletters. Sheldon Adelson (producer of the largest industry trade show, COMDEX, and other computer industry conferences) publishes the trade show daily newspapers and sells tapes and printed compendia of the seminars given at COMDEX. As an additional cash-generating channel, Adelson recently formed a travel and tour management company that brings people to COMDEX and the other conferences.

If you are in the service business, now is a good time to create a publishing channel, which you can launch on customers' advance payments. The function of the publication is to index the myriad issues in the industry on a monthly basis, to generate advertising dollars, and to locate new customers for your principal service.

USING 900 NUMBERS AND ONE-CALL POLLING

There are several recent innovations in telecommunications to help you learn more about your customers' needs and wants. This market research is paid for by the customer, which helps your cash flow. AT&T offers the "Dial-It 900 Service" ("976" for local calls), which handles large numbers of simultaneous calls to your company at a flat rate of 50 cents for the first minute and 30 cents per minute thereafter. Newspapers such as *USA Today* use the 900 service to survey readers' opinions on burning issues; then they print the results of the polls the following day. Manufacturers enclose an announcement of the 900 service in the packages their products are sold in and encourage customers to call with their comments. Customers do call, the manufacturers describe additional products, services, or contests or ask a series of preformulated questions in order to get more information about their customers. Ralston-Purina Company uses the 900 service for its "Great American Dog" contest, and Quaker Oats uses it so that children who eat its oatmeal can call to hear a prerecorded message from a well-known teddy bear.

One-call polling, a new service developed in 1987 by Creative Communications Associates (CCA) in New York, permits companies to tape five thousand simultaneous outgoing calls to businesses and households. The calls are in the form of decision trees, and the respondents give touch-tone responses. Bedras Bedrusian, CCA's president, proclaims the value of the service for polling, market research, and promotions. For CCA, the service is less expensive than sending out five thousand direct-mail questionnaires.

You can use the Dial-It 900 Service or one-call polling as entirely new distribution channels for locating new customers, asking them questions, determining their interest in your established products, taking their credit card numbers, and filling their orders, all without hiring any new sales personnel. Further, with the 900 service, the customer pays for the connect time to your company's prerecorded message. Say you manufacture Cajun and Creole sauces that are sold through supermarkets. Add a few lines of type to the labels, describing your 900 dial-in service for cooking tips. Then prepare a prerecorded message that offers a Cajun/Creole cookbook for $9.95; a stock pot for boiling chicken and shrimp, as described in the cookbook, for $12.95; and a free tin of cayenne pepper or an apron with every order of $25 or more. Then ask the customer for his or her name, address, and credit card number. C'est formidable! You have used the customer's money to generate a new source of cash for your company, and you did not pay for employees, advertising, or postage. The Dial-It 900 Service is an entirely new sales channel with immense cash-generating potential.

USING DIRECT-MAIL MARKETING

No other business is quite as easy to enter as direct-mail marketing, as demonstrated by all of the shop-by-mail catalogs you are offered.

Underline this section and write "regional downturn" in the margin, because one of the best new businesses to launch in a depressed region is a direct-mail catalog firm that offers the unique products of the area to tourists who have chosen to stay away. Santa Fe, New Mexico, is a popular summertime and ski-season tourist area, but in the February-to-June dog days, the artifact and art merchants have lean times. A direct-mail catalog that advertises their wares could generate cash flow during the tough months. The local merchants can provide you with color photographs of their products plus a list of sizes, colors, and prices, and they can pool their mailing lists to give the direct mailer thousands of prospects. Your costs of entering the business will be modest—printing and postage. The direct-mail business is going electronic as well, so that owners of personal computers can log onto hundreds of catalogs then order their products via mail, courier, or United Parcel Service.

Direct mail or mail order is the fastest growing segment of retailing. It is a $150-billion-per-annum business, and it represents about 15 percent of total annual retail sales.

USING VIDEOLOGS

With the cost of postage rising every few years, direct-mail marketers are beginning to turn to videotaped catalogs, or videologs for short. Home Video Marketplace (HVM) in Laguna Hills, California, published a thirty-eight-minute videolog in 1987 featuring twenty-nine products ranging in price from $25 to $6,500. Randy Richards, HVM's president, convinced three thousand video stores to stock the videolog, and it is beginning to sell. He reports the average order size as $150.

Some manufacturers are producing their own videologs. Royal Silk Manufacturing Company mails its videologs to some people and its printed catalog to others. Royal Silk has received average orders from videolog recipients that are 40 percent higher than the average orders from catalog recipients.

The drawback to videologs is their price. It costs about $25,000 to prepare a good fifteen-minute videotaped message and $7 to $10 to package and distribute each copy. Yet for fairly complicated products, a videotape can give more detail than a printed message. Since 1984, IBM has been using video marketing to encourage customers to trade up to newer products. Life Fitness, a marketer of computerized exercise equipment, introduced its new products with a fifteen-minute videotape. Durango Cookery in Austin, Texas, is introducing a new barbecue system with a variety of modular features. Rather than employ a sales force, Durango hired DWJ Associates in New York to prepare a fifteen-minute videotape. Durango mails the tape to potential dealers, to hardware stores, and to utility companies that have retail stores.

Jack Miller is president of Quill Corporation in Lincoln-shire, Illinois, a $200 million (revenues) direct-mail marketer of office products. Miller is giving serious consideration to videolog selling. With home VCRs already installed in 48.3 million households, and with projections of having fifty-six million installed by 1990, Miller believes videologs are an important secondary distribution channel.

If your company sells a product to households or on a business-to-business basis, begin considering videologs for marketing. Your sales force makes one-shot calls, whereas videotapes can be played over and over. Videotapes leave a lasting message, and you can mail videologs to five thousand customers, offer them the 900 service for placing the orders, or use one-call polling to answer queries and to ask for the check. With repeated calling, the orders will pour in; your new high-tech distribution channel could be pulling as many sales as your entire sales force.

USING JOINT VENTURES

Joint ventures are a frequently overlooked distribution channel, and they can create cash quickly. A *joint venture* is a partnership of two or more entities formed to undertake a certain project. A joint venture opportunity exists when each partner brings to the project a property that the other partners do not have but that they regard as integral to the success of the project.

A business in search of cash must honestly confront the fact that more than money is necessary to launch a new company. Although the project may call for manufacturing or distributing a certain product, merely obtaining capital does not make the company the most efficient manufacturer or the most successful distributor.

You may have an elegant and innovative product ready to roll out to the marketplace, but you may lack both the cash and the "feet on the street" to sell it. A large corporation may have manufacturing space available and a large sales force looking for new products. This situation cries out for a joint venture: a fifty-fifty enterprise that you manage for cash upfront and an ongoing management fee. We frequently see joint ventures in large-scale projects such as mining, aerospace, and telecommunications. Honda Motor Company introduced the moped through U.S. bicycle shops that later became its automobile dealerships. When your company is long on innovation and short on the means of getting it to market, think up an elegant joint venture, as did Sochiro Honda.

USING SHARED MAIL MARKETING

If you are currently mailing catalogs or direct-mail brochures to potential customers, there is an uncontrollable factor, known as rising postal rates, that must be a constant source of concern. Any uncontrollable variable is worrisome, but relying on the U.S. Postal Service to handle your mailing efficiently, together with facing the problem of ever-rising postal rates, is a migraine. To offset these costs, entrepreneurs have been popping up over the last ten years with shared mail marketing schemes. Your literature gets to the intended recipient, but it arrives in a package containing other brochures as well. Not only do you cut your costs by two-thirds, but the other offerings, if carefully chosen, enhance the sale of your product. Shared mail marketing is a terrific cost saver, and the several shared mail marketing companies presently in operation are apparently able to work closely with the U.S. Postal Service to assure delivery.

Advo Systems in Hartford, Connecticut, was founded by Jack Valentine in the late 1960s. It was a lackluster direct-mail service company that put the addresses of all of the nation's homes in its computers and performed huge mailings for its customers. Slugging it out toe-to-toe with R. R. Donnelly, Dun & Bradstreet, and other mass mailers was not Valentine's idea of a good time. He needed to do something unique with Advo's ninety million addresses. His team got the idea of bundling up to ten direct-mail pieces in a folder in order to reduce the cost of the mailer per customer.

Jay Engstrom left Advo Systems when it was acquired in 1986, and he started Marketing Publications Inc. in Westminster, California, a shared mail marketing firm that targets the corporate buyer. In less than two years, Engstrom's business-to-business one-million-piece monthly mailer has attracted several hundred customers, some of whom claim it is the best lead generator they have ever used. A second bundled mailer, "Affluent Lifestyles," goes out to 600,000 wealthy California homeowners each month and includes ten individual mailers. Marketing Publications represents a low-cost means of saving cash and generating sales. To his credit, Engstrom's new company exceeded $5 million in revenues in its second full year of operation.

If your company is in the printing business or if it mails a great deal of material every day, it is possible that you could offer a piggy-back mailing service to other companies that wish to reach the same market but lack the money. These other companies can contribute their mailing lists to a merged list, and for a small fee, you can agree to print and mail their literature. If ten of you get together, the costs of direct mail will drop appreciably, and moreover, you will have turned a cost area into a profit center.

Using Cable TV Marketing

Home shopping via cable is big business, aggregating $1.2 billion in 1986 and, by all accounts, rising. Syndications buy blocks of time on the home shopping cable channels and resell them to investment advisors, jewelry merchants, apparel manufacturers, and hair restoration companies. It might cost your company $40,000 per half hour to talk about your product line, but you can lay off part or all of that cost with advertisers.

The viewing audience for cable TV home shopping is similar to the readership of the *National Enquirer.* Although fascinated by the sensational, the audience is primarily interested in self-improvement: losing weight, regaining good health, and making money. They will purchase a unique cure, a diet plan, a penny stock gambit, or a how-to videotape program that they see being discussed by satisfied customers on the home shopping show. They would not be watching that particular channel in the first place unless they were open to buy something. After selling some of the thirty minutes to noncompetitive advertisers, you might be able to reduce your out-of-pocket expense to $10,000. Then, assuming your product sells at retail for $40, you need sell only 250 units to break even and only one thousand units to generate $30,000 in positive cash flow (excluding the cost of the product).

If the viewing audience is rated at one million households, a 2-percent response would be twenty thousand orders. However, before plunging into a $10,000 to $40,000 dice roll, ask the network's officers for references with whom you can talk in order to see how well this media will work for you.

FRANCHISING

When your company is being backed into a corner and must raise cash quickly, it may be too late to think of franchising. After all, in order to properly launch a franchising company, you need to hire counsel, draft a franchise prospectus, and file the prospectus with the states in which you wish to sell the franchises. That is the way it is supposed to be done; that is not the way it is usually done.

A case in point is Harold Otto, founder of the Wiks'n Stiks chain of candle stores. In 1976 Harold Otto had an idea that a small retail store specializing in freshly dipped, colorful, special purpose candles might be a franchisable concept, and he decided to test it. While waiting for a Houston mall developer to prepare his first store, Otto heard that someone across town wanted to buy a franchise. Otto took a check for $7,500 before he had built the model store. The Wiks 'n Stiks chain has grown to revenues of $61.3 million and to net profits of $560,000 after taxes, and in 1986, it achieved an initial public offering that valued the company at $36 million.

Franchising is first and foremost a financing method. It is not a particularly efficient product distribution system, and most of the profitable franchises are acquired back by the franchisor to enhance the value of the franchisor's common stock. The first franchise was sold by I. W. Singer, inventor of the sewing machine. In 1886, Singer granted a territorial dealership to a tool distributor in Ohio, and the tool distributor was selling more sewing machines than Singer could produce. In order to switch the dealer's payments so that Singer received them before the sale was made instead of after the sale was made—in order for Singer to get the cash to produce the product—Singer sold the Ohio dealer a franchise. The dealer gained territorial exclusivity to a very popular product, and Singer gained upfront financing.

Your retail concept, if unique, is replicable in other markets. If your operations manual is thorough and self-explanatory, and if you have an employee who can train someone in implementing the business, then you have something that will generate cash quickly. The legal blessing can come after you have generated some cash to stay afloat. However, avoid those states with the stiffest franchising regulations, such as Virginia, California, Ohio, and New York, until your legals are in order.*

If you do not want to franchise your retail business, you might franchise or license parts of it, such as special foods, recipes, tradenames. If you have a well-known tradename in salad dressing (such as Winn Schuler's of St. Joseph, Michigan) or a renowned cocktail sauce (such as Arnaud's of New Orleans, Louisiana), you might license other restaurants to use the product. They would have to buy it from you and pay in advance for the first shipment.

Franchising can also bring cash in a different way. You might consider the nation's thirty-five million franchise locations as potential customers for your product. They frequently

* Dennis L. Foster, *The Complete Franchising Book* (Rocklin, Calif.: Prima Publishing, 1988).

run contests and offer prizes and premiums to bring in customers, and they may want to use your product as a prize or premium.

USING DATABASE MARKETING

What better time than during a calamitous recession or a sales downturn to rethink your marketing methods? Do you really know much about your customers? Why do they buy from you? Who are they? If you knew more about them, two things would occur: first, you would be able to sell them more products; second, your customer list would become inestimably more valuable.

Companies such as Lexi International in Los Angeles are offering database research services; they employ artificial intelligence software to scan customer questionnaires that have been filled in by telemarketers, thereby generating answers to gut-level questions: Why does the customer buy your product but have it serviced elsewhere? Does a service customer trade up where he gets service, or does he return to you to trade up? What are the problems your customer encounters with your service department?

The cost of marketing goes up inexorably, but database marketing can generate vastly higher response rates to mailing lists or to customer calls because you know more about the customer you are calling on. Further, what if database marketing revealed that one-third of your product sales were to people—in businesses or households—who play tennis? You could share a catalog or videolog mailing piece with a tennis product marketer. Or you could acquire a tennis products supplier. You cannot catch black marlin with a worm hanging on a ten-ounce line. How you bait the hook will determine the size of the fish you catch.

LEARNING ABOUT USER GROUPS

If the product or system that your company produces is proprietary, is unique, is multipurpose, and is used in multiple environments, as was the microcomputer when it first came on the marketplace, form user groups. These are regional groups of customers who come together occasionally, perhaps every three months, to network with other users and to discuss the product—how to use it, how to incorporate new applications for it, and so on. The customers get lots of problems solved by networking with other users, thus saving you personnel costs. And further, developers of peripheral equipment are sometimes invited to user group meetings to demonstrate which of their products' features expand your product's capabilities. The advantages of your forming user groups are several:

1. The users pay to attend the meeting
2. User networking reduces the size of your service staff
3. Market research is gathered inexpensively
4. Some of your users will produce new peripheral equipment that you might be able to acquire or adapt

Two other hints: (1) tape the user group meeting on audio cassette and sell the cassettes for $12.95 each as "Proceedings of the User Group Meeting" to customers who could not attend; and (2) begin a user group newsletter, offer it free to customers, fill it with applications news, and solicit advertising from manufacturers and service companies that wish to reach your customers. Companies that could benefit from user groups include business product manufacturers, telecommunication systems companies, medical equipment manufacturers, service franchises, dealership organizations, aerobics and fitness product manufacturers, and recreational product manufacturers. In the event of a cash crunch, think up a variety of payment schemes to be implemented through the user group; tell them there is no time like the present to upgrade, to add features, to trade, or to introduce you to other potential customers.

BRAINSTORMING CRAZY IDEAS
TO GET YOU THINKING

Generating cash by daring to try new things can be a real high. Thus, while your mind is buzzing with new ideas for selling everything that isn't nailed down, here is a crazy idea for you: the going-out-of-business business. I am perhaps citing an extreme example, but the message is not extreme; it is readiness.

The business is simplicity itself: you help merchants in a certain community unload slow-moving inventory by taking it on consignment; renting a downtown, street-level store for two months; arranging the merchandise on tables and racks; and then plastering the windows with huge, handmade, "GOING OUT OF BUSINESS" signs. The merchandise is sold for 33 percent off retail—perhaps more toward the end of the sale—and you split the cash—no credit cards, please—fifty-fifty with your suppliers.

The business works well with apparel, but it could work nicely for sporting goods, tools, and home furnishings. You can move from town to town organizing sixty-day going-out-of-business sales. Or you can remain in your community and do it there continuously. Shoppers forget the business that was originally in the spot you rent, and when they see "GOING OUT OF BUSINESS" signs, they think, "No wonder they are going out of business; I never even knew they were there." Then they walk into the store to look for bargains.

When companies face a cash crisis, they respond entrepreneurially by using primitive business methods that generate the most upfront cash in the shortest period of time. To do this, they place the burden on the customer to generate cash in advance of delivery. In this manner, crude though it may appear, the company makes itself ready to take the next step in resolving its crisis.

SUMMARY

When I go into a company to do a work-out, I tell the president and the senior officers, "Get rid of the sacred cows. You are no longer in the such-and-such business. You're in the survival business, and the rules are different. First, we sell everything that you do not absolutely need, and we sell it for cash. Second, we buy time. We need six months to reorganize, and only cash will buy us time." If the management team has been backed by venture capitalists who have turned tail and run, they are probably in the denial stage—"This surely can't happen to us"—or the anger stage—"those sons of bitches better put up some more money"—but rarely are they in a realistic stage. They think that if they just had more marketing money, they could dig themselves out with cash from product sales. That will not happen.

Management teams not backed by venture capital are usually more realistic. Having bootstrapped themselves all the way, they never believed in the tooth fairy, and they have more street smarts, more intuition, about various ways of raising cash. While the manager backed by venture capital is talking to a Cayman Islands money finder who will deliver a commitment from a "prime international lender" for a $25,000 commitment fee, the street-smart manager is on the phone with seven schleppers, six barter guys, five licensing candidates, four partnerships that do sale-leasebacks, three list brokers, two asset-based lenders, and the ad manager for the user group newsletter.

This is what it takes. Turn your energy away from the business you were in and toward the survival business.

I have given you over twenty ways to generate cash by selling something, all of which you can implement immediately, and some of them dovetail neatly while shifting the costs to the customer. For instance, by putting your products into a shared videolog and asking viewers to call you on a 900 number, you can (1) generate sales through a new channel, (2) generate a higher average sales ticket, (3) learn more about your customer via a touch-tone questionnaire, and (4) generate a more valuable customer list to rent to others. This could permit you to lay off some sales personnel, thereby freeing up space to rent to a complementary business. In this way, you will generate a pile of cash to carry you through your redirect-and-grow plan.

Chapter Four

Buy Something

In hard economic times, many of your closest competitors will be more frightened than you are. They will see the glass half empty when you see it half full. They will fear a personal nightmare that includes losing their homes, pulling their children out of college, and pawning their wives' jewelry. Stories of the Great Depression that were told to them by their fathers will haunt their dreams, and they will awake in a cold sweat. Your absence of fear and your reliance on forecasting crises will create opportunities for you to generate cash by buying out your competitors and other troubled companies. Here's a true story from the last deep recession to help you understand this strategy.

A COMPANY IN TROUBLE

Harry and Phil Goodman (not their real names) inherited an $84 million (sales) drug, health, and beauty aid distribution company from their father in early 1974. They paid him $2 million, which "Dad" borrowed from the company's traditional bank by pledging the company's assets. Then Dad and Mom retired to Miami.

Harry and Phil—the "boys" as they had been called for the twenty-five years that they worked for Dad—began making all the key decisions, and the business remained reasonably stable for about a year. When the recession of 1975 hit, the boys went down to the company's bank to obtain a line of credit. They overcollateralized the line of credit, but unfortunately for them, they did not know it.

Accounts receivable and inventory, all of it in finished goods, aggregated $20 million, which would normally support borrowings of approximately $13 million; the building, trucks, vans, forklifts, and other equipment would permit another $2 million of debt, using conventional borrowing ratios of the asset-based lending industry. But the boys did not know of asset-based lenders or of commercial finance companies. Dad had always borrowed at one bank, and that is where the boys went to obtain a revolving credit. They came away with $5 million in loans, including the $2 million loan to buy out Dad, by pledging the company's accounts receivables, inventory, buildings, and equipment—the works. Dad's contacts had long since retired, and the banker was a young lady sporting a new MBA degree. When she asked Harry and Phil to sign personally and to provide their homes as side collateral, the boys willingly agreed to do it. This is what Dad must have done, they thought—then the 1975-76 Khoumeni recession hit.

By the time the prime rate had shot up to 21 percent, Harry and Phil had drawn the full amount of the line, and the company's profits went to pay $80,000 per month in interest fees. The boys began to panic. One night, Harry's wife awoke to hear her husband crying into his pillow. She shook him and said, "Harry, Harry. What is it?"

Harry wiped his eyes, walked her into the kitchen and poured each of them a glass of Scotch. He told his wife that he had signed personally for $5 million in loans and that he did not think the business would be able to repay the debt. Harry looked at his wife and said, "I think we could lose the house, your jewelry ... I think we could lose everything."

Harry's wife responded immediately with a reflex solution: "In the morning, we're going to see my cousin George the bankruptcy lawyer."

The next morning, George heard the story, saw the anguish in his cousin's face, and without analyzing the financial condition of the company, put the company into Chapter XI.

A smart businessman—let's call him Dan—had been routinely placing an advertisement in the *National Bankruptcy Journal*, a weekly newspaper read by bankruptcy lawyers who review changes in the bankruptcy code, rulings on important cases, changes in judgeships, and other trade information. The advertisement read as follows:

ATTENTION BANKRUPTCY LAWYERS

Our team can rescue your client's company, turn it around, add capital, develop a workable plan of reorganization and bring it out of Chapter XI. No front-end fees. Contact P.O. Box _____.

George, the bankruptcy lawyer, saw the advertisement, and with Harry's and Phil's approval, he contacted Dan. Dan asked to see the company's latest unaudited financial statements. Upon reviewing them, he smiled broadly then telephoned George to say that he would be in the area on other business during the next week and that he would be able to drop by to meet Harry and Phil. Dan knew the company would support greater borrowings. He understood that asset-based lenders frequently preferred to provide secured loans to companies in Chapter XI as part of their plan of reorganization because all other lenders were stopped from placing liens on the borrower's assets. What Dan did not know was how much debt the company's cash flow could support. He would have to see how badly Harry and Phil were managing things.

In George's office a few days later, Dan interviewed two terribly nervous men. Paralyzed with fear, Harry and Phil were unable to think of anything except the possibility of losing their personal assets. They had not spoken with any creditors, most of whom were shipping on COD terms and were growing concerned due to lack of information. The only secured debt in the company was bank debt. As a result, the company was a perfect candidate for a turn-around; that is, the company had a large number of unsecured creditors, no significant leases, and only one secured creditor. Federal payroll withholding taxes were current on a prepetition as well as a postpetition basis. Sales and income taxes were also current. The company was too healthy to be in Chapter XI, but so are many.

Dan interviewed Harry and Phil for several hours. Finally he said in his most serious voice, "Gentlemen, you have gotten yourselves into a real mess. Yes, a real mess. I don't know if I can bail you out, but let me make some changes in my schedule so that I can stay overnight. I'll study your financial statements in my motel room. If I find a way to rescue you, then I will make you a proposal in the morning."

Dan did not have much analytical work to do that evening. The bank could readily be replaced by an asset-based lender. Banks are cash-flow lenders—that is, they seek repayment *first* from the borrower's cash flow—not asset-based lenders. Commercial finance companies and commercial finance divisions of commercial banks are asset lenders first and cash flow lenders *second*. If Dan could find an asset-based lender to replace the bank and to remove Harry's and Phil's personal guarantees and personal collateral, they might be sufficiently relieved either to pay Dan a large fee, to give him a large interest in the company, or both. Dan drafted an agreement calling for majority ownership because he believed that the company could grow. The substance of the agreement called for Dan to raise $8 million for the company, repay the $5 million of secured debt, remove all personal guarantees, and have $3 million in the bank. Dan's consideration would be a 51-percent ownership for raising fresh capital plus a 10-percent fee on all capital that he raised. Dan planned to locate a seasoned manager to run the company at a higher level of profitability, a level sufficient to pay interest and principal of $2 million per annum.

Dan studied financial statements that showed a company capable of earning $4 million per annum before interest and taxes, but it was now earning only $1.5 million. Over $2 million was being wasted each year on fat: too many employees, too many company cars, country club dues, vacations paid for by the business, and excess inventories. Excess inventories provided an opportunity to improve profits. Distribution businesses have a typical percentage of "outs"—that is, out-of-stocks. They can typically fill 94 percent of every order.

To fill 96 percent of every order, which the company was doing, meant keeping another 2 percent of inventory. In other words, about $500,000 in cash could be saved by working the "out" ratio down to 94 percent and special ordering those items to protect good customer relationships. Other operational changes were listed by the entrepreneur—they numbered over twenty-five—but he would save them for discussion with his chief executive officer candidate.

Dan returned to George's office in the morning and presented his proposal. He requested a sixty-day exclusive option to rescue the company, for which, if he succeeded, Dan wanted a 51-percent ownership, a 10-percent fee on all new capital raised, and the ability to manage the company as chief executive officer (or to choose one), which included the right to reduce costs, the right to hire and fire personnel, and any or all powers needed to generate cash flow sufficient to retire indebtedness under the plan of reorganization. George conferred privately with Harry and Phil and added only one change to Dan's contract: subject to the approval of the bankruptcy court. Dan accepted.

Four years later, Dan sold the company for $20 million, putting $10 million in the boys' pockets, before taxes. Harry and Phil joined their father in Miami, where all three men have gone into real estate development together. Dan made $8 million from the sale, and his chief executive officer made $2 million.

A knowledge of the distribution industry, the bankruptcy law, and the lending requirements of asset-based lenders generated a significant profit and a happy result from a situation that began with two frightened inheritors of a sound regional distribution business. (To find salvageable companies for yourself, subscribe to the *National Bankruptcy Reporter,* published by Andrews Publications, 5123 Westchester Pike, Edgemont, Pennsylvania 19028.)

GATEWAY COMPUTER SYSTEMS

A more recent example of the successful takeover of a thriving business whose founders hastily placed it in Chapter XI is

Gateway Computer Systems, a $75 million (sales) computer retail chain with ten locations primarily in California.

Gateway was *Inc.*'s fourteenth fastest growing, privately held company in 1985, more than doubling its sales each year from 1982 to $75 million in 1985. In 1985 Gateway received several offers to merge, to take in private capital, or to go public. Each offer to take the company public, acquire it, or invest in it was rejected by Gateway's board of directors, and Gateway was growing faster than its ability to pay its creditors in a timely manner. In August 1985, IBM Corporation threatened to raise the price at which it sold computers to Gateway if the company did not bring its accounts current.

Gateway hired Paine Webber Corporation to raise $4 million for the company via a private placement. Paine Webber elicited the interest of Lincoln National Investment Management Corporation, which agreed to invest $2.5 million of the required $4 million. Two million dollars went immediately to IBM Corporation. Several months later, Gateway slipped back into serious cash flow problems and began scrambling desperately for a merger partner.

A promoter visited Gateway's president and majority stockholder and recommended a strategy for going into Chapter XI, settling indebtedness for cents on the dollar (thereby increasing net worth), acquiring some other computer retailers, and emerging from Chapter XI a stronger and healthier company. The promoter's story persuaded the Gateway board. Gateway filed for protection in July 1986, but the promoter was unable to convince the creditor's committee (which was headed by Lincoln National's attorney) to back his plan of reorganization.

In the early fall of 1986, Rick Meadows and Rick Selvage (two work-out entrepreneurs from Columbus, Ohio) approached the creditor's committee with a plan they liked. For 51-percent ownership of Gateway and the chief executive officer's power, they would invest $1 million and provide lines of credit through Selvage's electronics distribution company, aggregating $1.5 million. The plan was approved by the bankruptcy court in mid-1987. Gateway has been successfully turned around, and all previous investors have been diluted by one-half. Gateway's sales were expected to return to $75 million in 1987 with a healthy bottom line, and Meadows and Selvage stand to make more than ten times their investment within three years.

BUYING A COMPANY WITH YOUR TROUBLED COMPANY

"When you're broke buy something," is the clarion call of the work-out entrepreneur. As Bill Tauscher and Richard Bard did when their insolvent Lag Drug acquired the thriving Fox Vliet Drug to create the beginnings of $3 billion FoxMeyer Corporation, you too can use the carcass of your insolvent company to acquire your way to genuine liquidity. The assets you have to work with are the following:

1. Your suppliers. They do not want to lose the money that your company owes them, and they will make concessions in order to get their money back.
2. Tax loss carry forward. Although diminished in value by the Tax Reform Act of 1986, you can still shelter some of the earnings of the company you buy with your company's tax loss carry forward.

There are optimal and suboptimal credit configurations for the company that is seriously close to bankruptcy. The best candidate for a Chapter XI is the company with (1) one large, secured creditor that would suffer a serious loss if the company did not repay its debt, and (2) hundreds of unsecured creditors with amounts substantially larger than the average debt. A bad candidate is the company with (1) no creditors or only a few secured creditors, and (2) unsecured assets available for other creditors to grab. The absolute worst candidate has a handful of large, secured creditors and very few small, unsecured creditors. In the latter circumstance, the large secured creditors will be impatient with the company's plan of reorganization and will attempt to force the company into Chapter VII— involuntary bankruptcy—in order to have the assets sold and their debts paid. In the best circumstance, the secured creditors are protected in the event of Chapter VII, but the unsecured creditors will encourage a plan of reorganization, which gets them paid. The unsecured creditors become allies of the company's management or replacement management: anyone who can implement the plan of reorganization that gets them paid. The attitude of most unsecured creditors to a person offering them a plan of reorganization is, "I wouldn't accept the plan if there were an option, but because there is no option, count me in."

Tauscher and Bard realized that outside of Chapter XI, Lag Drug Company was hopelessly insolvent. But in Chapter XI, the company would be solvent; it would have time to reorganize its debts. In Chapter XI, the unsecured creditors become partners of the debtor.

The pharmaceutical, health, and beauty aids industry has witnessed so many bankruptcies that it owns a small auditorium on Lexington Avenue in New York City where its credit managers may be addressed by debtors. When Tauscher and Bard put Lag Drug Company into Chapter XI, they were strongly urged to come to New York to take the stage. This was a first for all three of us. Our average age was 32, and we faced an audience of approximately thirty credit managers whose average age was 55 and whose average account receivable with Lag was about $400,000. Pfizer's credit manager was there, as were Clairol's, Richardson-Merrill's, Merck's, Upjohn's, R. J. Reynolds's, American Tobacco's, and more. We feared the worst.

Tauscher sat in the center with Bard and me on either side; we were his numbers men. The 29-year-old, youthful looking, six-foot-four-inch Tauscher told the angry creditors the truth. He was hired by Lag's president to set up the IBM System 36 computer that he had sold the company a few months earlier. He put all the customer records, inventory, payroll records, and accounts payable on the computer. When the president died suddenly, Tauscher was the only one who understood the company, and Bard was its secured lender. The owners of Lag Drug asked Tauscher to become its president, and he asked Bard to join him as chief financial officer. I had been asked to raise venture capital to turn the company around, and I had found several interested investors. The creditors squirmed in their seats with obvious disbelief. They had heard lots of stories from this stage over the years, but three young men, still wet behind the ears, had just told them something they normally laugh about at the nineteenth hole.

Tauscher continued. "Our plan to get you repaid is to acquire Fox Vliet Drug Company in Wichita, Kansas. We can raise the purchase price by borrowing on Fox Vliet's assets and by using the venture capital that we have raised, and we will repay the indebtedness out of Fox Vliet's cash flow."

The creditors exploded. "You're going to trash one of our healthy customers?" they asked. "You're going to put two of our customers in bankruptcy?" they screamed. "What kind of story is this?"

But we held to our story. "If you gentlemen want to get your $12 million back, you've got to help us. You're going to have to help us buy Fox Vliet," Tauscher said.

"You're going to hock Fox Vliet to the gills, stretch us out on $24 million in debt, and ask us to keep shipping to you and to wish you well?" the Pfizer credit manager asked.

"That is what we're asking you to do. That is our plan of reorganization. We want you to go along with us," Tauscher said.

The meeting ended, but not the drama. The seller had to be held in place, and he had set a deadline of December 29. The secured lender in the leveraged buy-out had to be convinced that the financing would happen, but Bard was experienced at speaking with asset-based lenders. The venture capitalists were the toughest group to hold in line bcause they were backing two young men with no track record who were financing out of Chapter XI. The owners of Lag Drug Company had to agree to suffer 80-percent dilution in order to permit a rescue of their company. Finally, the secured creditors had to approve the plan of reorganization. Tauscher, Bard, and I acted like boys with their fingers in the dike, except that there were many holes in many dikes.

The Lag Drug/Fox Vliet deal was one of the first leveraged buy-outs and easily the first bankruptcy LBO. It happened because Tauscher realized he could leverage the suppliers. He did this by communicating with them, by gaining their confidence, and by making them believers.

Two years after the closing, the venture capitalists squeezed Tauscher's equity down to such a small amount that he walked out of the company. When FoxMeyer began to cough blood like a harpooned whale on the beach, the venture capitalists begged Tauscher to rejoin the company. He did so on his terms and nurtured FoxMeyer to sales of $3 billion, the second largest drug, health, and beauty aid distributor in the country. In 1987, the venture capitalists backed Tauscher and Bard in their acquisition of Computerland Corporation.

Some Facts about Chapter XI

The FoxMeyer strategy relied heavily on the use of Chapter XI as a haven from lawsuits in order to develop and implement a redirect-and-grow plan. Let us examine some of the characteristics that could make Chapter XI an interesting strategy for your company, should it fall on hard times. The Federal Bankruptcy Code was radically amended in 1985 to make life easier for debtors and more difficult for creditors. Gone forever is Chapter X, the old involuntary bankruptcy. It has been replaced by Chapter VII, which involves wind-up and liquidation for the benefit of creditors by a court-appointed trustee.

Chapter XI is a shelter, allowing the debtor to remain in possession for many months or several years while reorganizing—that is, while developing a plan that is acceptable to all classes of creditors and emerging from Chapter XI in good financial health. As evidence of Chapter XI rising in importance and status, law firms are actively recruiting bankruptcy specialists, the attendance at legal conventions on bankruptcy is growing at a rate of 40 percent per annum,* and the number of bankruptcy filings per annum has increased from 185,000 in 1980 to 376,000 in 1985.

* S. L. Mintz, "Sifting for Values," *Corporate Finance* (December 1987).

UNPAID PAYROLL TAXES   If your company files for protection with federal withholding taxes owing—and as you know, cash-deprived companies frequently fail to pay these taxes—there is no settling with the Internal Revenue Service (IRS). The full amount is owed when you emerge from Chapter XI; however, the IRS gives you six years to repay the debt.

Are you liable for these taxes if the company cannot pay them? The answer is yes if your name is on the signature card for the payroll account and if you were in direct control of that account. Thus, a chief executive officer who does not sign the payroll checks and who does not directly control those people who do is probably not liable for unpaid federal and state withholding taxes.

The worst scenario is when a company goes into Chapter VII (liquidation of assets rather than reorganization) unable to pay its obligation to the IRS, and the IRS comes after the CEO, the chief financial officer, and the members of the board of directors. There is bad news and good news. First, the bad news: the IRS will garnishee 10 percent of your salary for the rest of your life, or until it is paid in full. Now, the good news: you can have only one garnishee at a time. So if you see this event coming, remember that the IRS will have to wait in line if another garnishment is filed ahead of it.

Say that you are in Chapter XI, that your business turns down, and that you are unable to pay postpetition payroll taxes, in addition to prepetition taxes. Does the IRS exile you to a leper colony? No. The rule is that the plan of reorganization, in order to be acceptable to this class of creditor, must include payment in full of postpetition taxes upon emerging from Chapter XI.

CRAM DOWN PROVISION   The creditors of a company in bankruptcy are arranged into classes according to the priority of their claims. The priority class of creditor includes the IRS and administrative claims—that is, legal bills from your bankruptcy lawyer and others who have been approved by the bankruptcy court to do work for your Chapter XI company. These must be paid in full in order to emerge from Chapter XI or Chapter VII. Fully secured creditors are next in line, and lenders usually fill this category. The third class is partially secured creditors, or those with "impaired" collateral; it is important to have an ally in this class. Finally, there is the unsecured class of creditors, those without any collateral.

Fifty percent of all creditors and two-thirds of each class of creditor must approve the debtor's plan of reorganization before the company is permitted to emerge from Chapter XI. It is the nature of some creditors to continually reject the plans of reorganization submitted by the debtor. Recalcitrant creditors feel that if they keep leaning on the company to improve its plan, the company will indeed do so. They are right in some cases; they are nit-picking nuisances in others.

The authors of the 1987 Bankruptcy Code must have felt that nit-picking nuisances should be punished, because they introduced the "cram down" provision. If at least one impaired creditor—that is, partially secured or unsecured creditor— accepts the plan of reorganization, the bankruptcy court can cram it down the throats of all creditors. Thus, virtually any reasonable plan of reorganization will be approved by the court if the debtor persuades one impaired creditor to accept. How might you do this? You must pay that creditor promptly and efficiently while in Chapter XI, showing that creditor your good faith and your attention to its needs.

GO PUBLIC Yes, you can go public via a Chapter XI filing. The expression once applied to companies that save their lives by an initial public offering—"go broke *or* go public"—has become obsolete. It is now possible to "go broke *and* go public." The new Bankruptcy Code provides that creditors may be offered stock in settlement of their claims. Moreover, the stock is exempt from registration under the Securities and Exchange Act of 1933, which means that the stock is *free trading* (the holder can sell it through his broker the minute he receives it). This creates an extraordinary opportunity for troubled companies to raise cash.

Why might you want to issue stock to creditors? First, it saves cash and enhances the company's liquidity. Second, if debt is replaced with equity, the company's net worth increases.

Third, much of the stock will be dumped at distress prices, and you or your key employees might be able to buy up stock (issued as one share for each one dollar of debt) at 16 cents or less per share. Fourth, if the company's story is a good one, upon its emergence from Chapter XI, the stock will rise in price, and in two years the insiders—you, your key employees, and your investors under 10 percent—can sell some stock to create personal wealth.

Compumed was founded in 1983 by Robert O. Stuckelman, a former Litton Industries executive, and by Howard S. Mark, M.D., to rent electrocardiograph machines to physicians. Over 2,600 EKG machines were installed throughout the country and tied to Compumed's central computer in Los Angeles. Compumed charged its physician clients a rental fee and a processing fee. By 1985 the company was very profitable but highly leveraged due to $8 million in loans to buy the EKG machines. Compumed filed a registration statement with the SEC for an initial public offering, but the SEC told Compumed that it had been selling franchises without filing a prospectus with the SEC. The initial public offering was derailed, and Compumed filed for protection under Chapter XI. It was a classic Chapter XI—three large creditors and hundreds of unsecured creditors. Rental fees were sufficient to pay interest and operating expenses, but the company was prohibited by the SEC from placing more units in the field.

Because their clients' rental payments would run out in three years, Stuckelman and Mark felt that they could grow only if the company acquired other medical devices to sell or to rent to its 2,600 physician clients. To make acquisitions, Compumed would have to be public. Thus, it paid all unsecured creditors with stock, creating in the process a large net worth sufficient to obtain a NASDAQ listing. Moreover, because its expansion story was pretty well accepted by its new stockholders, there was not much selling of the stock. Compumed has roughly eight million shares of stock outstanding and was trading over-the-counter at about 25 to 50 cents per share in mid-1988.

Compumed is a perfect example of two axioms: (1) when you're broke, buy something; and (2) go broke to go public.

THE TAX LOSS CARRY FORWARD   Alas, the government giveth and the government taketh away. Whereas the Bankruptcy Code has been improved for debtors, the use of the tax loss carry forward to shelter the earnings of the company you acquire has lost much of its effectiveness. Prior to the Tax Reform Act of 1986, if the buyer had accumulated losses over the last few years and was acquiring a company that had earnings, the seller's earnings could be sheltered for five years by carrying the buyer's losses forward. For example, if the buyer had a $1 million loss in 1985 and acquired a company that produced a combined income of $1 million in 1986, there would be no tax payment on 1986 combined earnings.

But this privilege has been removed. What remains is as follows: the buyer multiplies the interest rate on seven-year government notes—say, 8 percent—by the acquisition price, and if the buyer indeed has losses, it can still carry them forward, but to a smaller degree. For example, using the above case and assuming an acquisition price of $1 million, the annual savings would be $80,000 per annum or 8 percent of the acquisition price.

Presumably, the positive feature of the tax loss carry forward was regarded as being helpful to corporate raiders while being hurtful to entrenched management, and the authors of the Tax Reform Act of 1986 were lobbied more aggressively by entrenched managements than by raiders.

Boneyard Buying

There are two thoughts bouncing around in this chapter: (1) in troubled times, you can walk through the corporate boneyard and buy ruined or merely frightened companies very inexpensively; and (2) if your company fails due to hard times, you can shut down all operations, lay off all personnel except the survival team, and acquire a healthy company via leveraged buyout financing techniques. The excitement in boneyard buying is being cheap, tight, penny-pinching, niggardly—throwing dimes on the table as if they were manhole covers. When asked by the seller's lawyer to improve the offer, say no. These are tough times and part of the reason that you and other companies are in trouble is that you said yes when you should have said no.

In boneyard buying, you don't know how much worse the economy might become. You are piling on mountains of debt to make an acquisition that in itself is speculative and uncertain, but the acquisition you are making is supposed to generate life-saving cash. Therefore, you must be so tight with your commitments, money, and guarantees that you squeak when you walk. If it is not your style to be tough and tight, then you probably won't survive hard times.

DIVISIONAL BUY-OUT

If you hear of a large corporation that is having problems, you might consider using LBO financing techniques to buy out one of its divisions. You can buy the division from the corporation by borrowing on the assets of the division and repaying the loans from the division's cash flow. To enhance cash flow, cost-saving steps will have to be taken. Your ace in the hole is that the parent corporation's administrative service charge will be eliminated. Non-related activities and assets can be spun off to raise additional cash. The parent corporation will frequently bend a little to help finance the buy-out if you spread some ownership among the division's managers.

The feasibility of accomplishing a divisional buy-out takes some quick math. To do this you must first apply conventional lending ratios used by asset-based lenders to the division's principal assets in order to determine how much money you can raise. This usually results in an *equity gap*—that is, a shortfall between the amount you can leverage and the probable asking price. That gap can be filled in a number of ways, as we shall see. The second calculation is to arrive at an *adjusted EBIT*— earnings before interest and taxes (remember this acronym!) that are adjusted for the division's cost savings once it is free from its parent and from the related corporate overhead charges. By cutting salaries and by tightening the belt in other ways, adjusted EBIT will go up accordingly. For the third calculation, divide annual debt service on the acquisition debt into the adjusted EBIT in order to ascertain whether there is sufficient cash flow (adjusted EBIT plus depreciation) to pay debt service while retaining something for you and your stockholders.

Let's put some numbers to this. Assume you spot a division whose balance sheet appears as shown in Table 4.1.

Conventional loan ratios used by asset-based lenders are 80 to 85 percent of the value of the accounts receivable that are less than ninety days outstanding, 50 percent of the value of raw materials and finished goods inventories, and 75 percent of the liquidation (auction or quick-sale) value of plant, machinery, and equipment. There may be other assets off the balance sheet that can be used as collateral. The principal ones are customer lists, technological know-how such as patents and copyrights, and leaseholds, as we discussed in Chapter 3.

Assuming that all of the accounts receivable are less than 90 days old and "qualified"—that is, acceptable to the lender—and assuming that two-thirds of the inventories are either raw materials or finished goods and that the net book value of the plant and equipment is equal to liquidation value, then the division manager can raise $3,320,000 in cash from the division's balance sheet (see Table 4.2).

From the $3,320,000 cash advance, we must deduct the $1,200,000 note payable, which will have to be repaid by the new lender (unless it is owed to the corporation and is taken

Table 4.1 *Balance Sheet of Divisional Buy-out Candidate*

Assets		Liabilities and Net Worth	
Current Assets		Current Liabilities	
Cash	$ 350,000	Accounts Payable	$ 900,000
Accounts		Accrued Expenses	250,000
receivable	2,450,000	Note Payable—Parent	1,200,000
Inventories	1,800,000	Stockholders' equity	3,350,000
Plant and			
equipment		Total Liabilities	
Net	850,000	and Net Worth	$5,750,000
Other assets	250,000		
Total Assets	$5,700,000		

Table 4.2   *Raisable Cash*

Source	Book Value	times	Loan Ratio	equals	Cash Advance
Accounts receivable	$2,450,000	×	0.85	=	$2,082,500
Inventories	1,200,000	×	0.50	=	600,000
Plant and equipment (net)	850,000	×	0.75	=	637,500
Total	$4,500,000				$3,320,000

back by the corporation as part of the purchase price). The net cash available to pay the corporation is $2,120,000, or to be safe, $2,050,000 after appraisal, legal, and accounting fees and after the lender's commitment fee.

Let's assume that the division's operating statement for the most recent twelve-month period appears as in Table 4.3.

To calculate adjusted EBIT, add the division's profits, $982,750, to the corporate surcharge, $810,000; then add the back interest expense, $200,000, and noncash charges and savings due to belt tightening, say $500,000. (The elimination of perks could be substantial.) In any event, let's assume that the adjusted EBIT is $2,502,550 per annum.

Table 4.3   *Twelve-Month Operating Statement of Divisional LBO Candidate*

Item	Percent of Sales	Dollar Amount
Sales	100.0	$ 13,500
Cost of goods sold	67.0	9,045,000
Gross Profit	33.0	4,455,000
Selling expense	10.0	1,350,000
General and administrative expenses	8.3	1,112,250
Corporate surcharge	6.0	810,000
Interest expense	1.5	200,000
Total Operating Expenses	25.8	3,472,250
Net Profit Contribution	7.2	$ 982,750

Is the adjusted EBIT large enough to cover the debt service? Assume the seller will hold the $1.2 million note at 16.7 percent interest and will accept the $2 million in cash that you offer as the down payment; another $1 million that you must raise outside; plus a $4 million, five-year note, secured by all of the assets in a second position to the asset-based lender at 15 percent annual interest. Further assume that the note amortizes at the rate of $400,000 per annum with a fifth-year balloon of $2 million. The total purchase price is $9,520,000. Let's see whether adjusted EBIT will support this massive amount of leverage. (See Table 4.4.)

Adding the total annual principal payment to the total annual debt yields the total annual debt service of $2,241,000, which is barely covered by the adjusted EBIT of $2,502,550. It is a "no hiccup" LBO—that is, if there is just one hiccup, such as a two-percentage-point increase in interest rates or a small reduction in earnings, the division's ability to service its debt will be doubtful.

There is some leeway in the deal. An asset-based lender could ask the selling corporation to guarantee the collectability of the accounts receivable. If the seller does so, the lender has the ability to loan 100 percent of the face amount of the accounts receivable. Second, the lender will probably ask you and your teammates, who will become stockholders, to guarantee the loan in proportion to the teammates' ownership. I will discuss the personal exposure of personal guarantees shortly. Let's just say that if you are signing a personal guarantee on $3 million for the first time in your life, it is your moment of truth.

Table 4.4 *Annual Debt Service of Divisional LBO Candidate*

Asset-Based Loans	Face Amount of Loans	times	Interest Rate	Interest equals	Annual Principal Expenses	Annual Payment
Revolving line	$2,682,500	×	.18	=	$ 483,000	—
PP&E loan	637,500	×	.18	=	115,000	$123,000
Existing note	1,200,000	×	.167	=	200,000	200,000
Seller's note	4,000,000	×	.18	=	720,000	400,000
Total	$8,520,000				$1,518,000	$723,000

Are you willing to risk all? Are your partners the ones you would choose as war buddies?

The $1 million that you must raise from outside sources can be obtained from LBO funds, which became extremely popular in the mid-1980s and which have provided over $25 billion from institutional investors in the form of equity gap, or mezzanine, financing.

Another way to improve the deal for you is to ask the corporation to take back the accounts receivable as part of the purchase price. Typically, the asset-based lender will not loan against the inventories if it does not tie up the accounts receivable. But in this instance, the face value of the accounts receivable is $2,450,000, and the initial take down on the accounts receivable and on the inventory line is $2,682,500. Thus, by having the seller keep the accounts receivable, you need to raise $232,000 more for the equity gap, but you save $593,000 in annual interest charges. Plus, your current assets can be used as backup collateral if you need capital in the future.

In this example, relatively high interest rates were used, on the assumption that the economy will be in a serious decline at the time you purchase your division. Indeed, interest rates could be five points higher, and the buy-out price could be $3 million higher, yet you could still make the purchase. That is the most exciting aspect of leveraged buy-outs: they are highly do-able with only a small amount of creative exertion.

There are asset-based lenders, mezzanine investors, and LBO-experienced lawyers and accountants who are specialists in buy-outs from boneyard to corporation divisions. They have helped many deal breakers get fixed and many remorseful sellers return to the table and make the deal happen. When you buy your division or any other company, hire experienced professionals. After all, you are implementing a survival strategy, and failure could be disastrous. Begin the buy-out by contacting one of these specialists whose names can be found in directories that are sold in large bookstores or that are made available in libraries. If your search proves fruitless, write me in care of the publisher.

It is smart to buy something when you are broke. That is why $25 billion in mezzanine capital has been pulled together in the United States since 1982—to help you effect a buy-out. And that is why ten times that amount, or $250 billion, in leverage is in the hands of skilled, asset-based lenders—to provide the bulk of the financing. Smart money moves to where the biggest profits are, and a quarter of a trillion dollars thinks there are big profits in buy-outs. Join the smart set and use the coming hard times to buy-out a competitor, a division, a healthy company, or a boneyard company. Prices are not going to get much better.

FACILITIES MANAGEMENT

You need not buy a company or a division to generate cash flow. Furthermore, if your skills are in the service area—data processing, health care, money management—acquiring an asset-rich business, one that can be leveraged to make the buy, may simply not be in the cards. To achieve the same result—upfront cash—you can sell a facilities management contract; that is, you can contract to operate a facility for the price of the facility's annual budget and a substantial upfront payment. Like an LBO, you can put up virtually no money and end up with a business that offers cash flow and wealth potential. It's smart. It's exciting. But you have to be Cool-Hand Luke to pull it off.

With increasing regularity, money managers are "buying" their divisions away from bank holding companies using facilities management contracts. Jack Favia, the former head of Chemical Bank's Trust Department, was one of the first to negotiate the right to manage a major bank's trust department in an independent company. The $9 billion that his firm, Favia, Hill & Company, manages earns about $500,000 in annual fees; plus Favia, Hill is free to seek other clients.

Data processing divisions of large corporations have been "bought" from their parent corporations as well. Computeristics was Uniroyal's data processing department but is now a stand-alone company doing work for Uniroyal and others.

The second stage in a facilities management "buy-out" is to take on new clients, in addition to the corporation; achieve increased earnings; then sell the business to the public or to a single buyer, which will result in wealth for the key employees.

Jennison Associates, a money management firm in New York City, is made up largely of former Chase Manhattan Bank trust department officers. It was acquired in 1987 by Equitable Life Assurance Society for approximately $36 million.

Money management divisions and data processing divisions of large corporations are not the only service departments that are subject to facilities management buy-outs. You can accomplish the same thing if you are in the human resources department, in corporate planning, in marketing, in the commissary, in transportation services, or in many other departments. The two young people who ran McKinsey & Company's library for several years negotiated a facilities management contract, permitting them to serve McKinsey and others in a new company called Find/SVP. An excellent example of facilities management contracts is the case of Corrections Corporation of America (CCA), which operates prisons under long-term contracts. Whereas the states seem to run prisons at a cost of $80 per prisoner per day, CCA can do it profitably at $40 per prisoner per day.

When buying your division via a facilities management contract, the key is in the negotiations. You have to know that you can run the facility less expensively than the current budget. When you walk in, your initial offer should be that the department's budget will not increase for the term of the contract, say five years, while the quality of the service will remain consistently high. In the depths of economic bad times, this could be music to the ears of a large corporation looking to get blood from a stone. But if that offer is inadequate, you will probably have to offer cost savings. So know in advance where you can make some cuts.

Facilities management was created and shaped by H. Ross Perot, founder of Electronic Data Systems (EDS). He sold lots of large IBM computers to several large Texas corporations and institutions in 1964. Then noticing that they were unable to process their general ledgers, accounts receivable, inventories, accounts payable, and payrolls, Perot left IBM, formed EDS, and offered to manage his customers' data processing facilities. The customers paid EDS their data processing budget for the year, and EDS assumed both the payroll costs and the equipment costs of the division. As EDS added customers, it laid off personnel, it sold excess equipment, and its bottom line became exceptionally large as a percentage of revenues.

No one else understood facilities management for at least five years because EDS did not advertise. Business came to the firm by word of mouth. In 1969, EDS made its initial public offering at the then unheard of price/earnings ratio of 115x, and soon EDS had competitors; Automatic Data Processing, Computer Sciences Corporation, and a division of General Electric Corporation entered the business.

Facilities management is becoming more popular as governments privatize. Government agencies faced with budgetary crises are selling some of their more costly departments such as sanitation and prisons to facilities management contractors. The federal government is planning to sell power generation and air-traffic control to private contractors. Day-care centers established in manufacturing companies are run by facilities management contractors such as Gymboree Corporation to permit working mothers to have more time with their children during the day.

TOUGH TIMES ARE GOOD TIMES FOR BUY-OUTS

Whether you're planning an LBO or a facilities management buy-out, if times are tough, remember that you are negotiating from strength, and offer to put up very little of your own money.

Look at Ronald Jackson, president and chief executive officer of Kenner Parker Toys in Beverly, Massachusetts. The fifth largest toy manufacturer in the United States, the company lost money as a subsidiary of General Mills Corporation and broke into the black one year after Jackson and his management team bought it for $350 million in an LBO. (See Table 4.5.)

General Mills was happy to unload Kenner Parker because its mainstay products, Care Bears and Star Wars items, were being discontinued with no blockbuster toys or games in development. After gaining its independence, Jackson slashed costs

Table 4.5 Kenner Parker Toys[a]

	1985	1986	Percent Change
Sales	$340	$503	48.0
Net Profit	(58)	25	142.8

[a]Amounts in thousands of dollars

(including advertising) from $49 million in 1985 to $36 million in 1986, while licensing Ghostbusters and SilverHawks to shore up revenues. Not long after going public, Kenner Parker was threatened by a takeover bid from New World Production, which owns the Marvel line of comic books and Superheroes. Jackson protected his independence by selling Kenner Parker to Tonka Corporation for an acquisition price of $628 million. Jackson, who doubled his money in two years, remains chief executive officer of Kenner Parker, which is nearly twice the size of Tonka.

WHEN LENDERS ASK FOR YOUR PERSONAL GUARANTEE

You may not be able to effect an LBO or finance your divisional buy-out without the lender (which could be the seller, if it takes your promissory note) asking for your personal guarantee. There are negotiating tactics that you can employ to lessen your exposure, but lenders were not born yesterday. They want your *touchas offentish*—which is Yiddish for "tusch on the table." Lenders may say it differently, but that is what they mean.

The first step in negotiating a less punitive personal guarantee is to make a strong case against a *joint and several* guarantee, in which each partner is personally liable for the full amount of the loan. If the loan is for $4 million and if you and your three partners are each jointly and severally liable, then each of you is liable for the full $4 million. As that is clearly overkill, a good case can be made for a *several* only—that is, your aggregate guarantees total $4 million.

Bruce Engel, CEO of WTD, is giving fits to Weyerhauser and other lumber mills in the Pacific Northwest. A bankruptcy lawyer and iconoclast, Engel's personal net worth in 1983 was $300,000, yet he personally guaranteed $500,000 of creditor obligations in order to acquire a bankrupt sawmill. If the sawmill failed, there was no way he could repay the IOU. But Engel took his bluff two steps further by persuading several backers to reschedule mortgage payments and by convincing one creditor to forego interest payments in exchange for a small percentage of the mill's monthly sales.

Engel was thrilled by the chance to prove himself. "Bruce came in as an outsider. Then he outperformed all the timber barons. And he just loves that," said Chad Brown, a forest-products analyst at Kidder Peabody & Company (which took WTD public last year, creating $80 million in personal wealth for Engel). Reviewing the mill's past, Engel decided to knock aside the most common practices of the business. "I saw an overmature industry with costs too high and productivity too low, a business that was still dominated by an incredibly damaging macho ethic."*

Engel had reason to blink soon after he turned the mill around. Just when he sank WTD's new capital into two additional mills, the lumber market suffered another chilling down draft. Engel did some calculations and realized that if he worked off the logs he had on hand at a manageable production rate, the company would lose hundreds of thousands of dollars in no time. So Engel faced down his suppliers and told them that he was shutting down two of his three mills and that he would not be able to pay them for three months. He also managed to squeeze more favorable terms from his creditors. The creditors cooperated, having seen the Engel ship sail through rough water once before.

If you have several nonactive partners, such as those who fill the equity gap and own 25 percent of the new company, you might be able to eliminate 25 percent of the loan guarantee. Your argument to the lender would be that because your ownership is only 75 percent of the enterprise, you should not be at

* Bruce Engle, *Success!* (December 1987), pp. 54-56.

risk for more than 75 percent of the loan. The deeper the recession and the more difficult the lender's ability to find good loan customers, the easier your negotiations will be to soften the personal guarantee.

SUMMARY

"When you're broke, buy something!" That is the fastest and most decisive way to get out of illiquidity. When companies in the portfolio of venture capital funds that I managed did not fulfill their business plans, I immediately stopped the businesses they were in and used their shells to buy LBO targets that had positive cash flow. There is an extraordinary amount of LBO debt and equity gap financing available to assist the buyer. Think about it for a moment. It may cost you $75,000 in accounting, legal, appraisal, and bank commitment fees to complete an LBO. But when it is accomplished, you own a business with positive cash flow, which can cover or compromise the debts of your original business.

Further, you can use LBO financing techniques to buy a frightened competitor, the division of a large and troubled corporation, or a company in your region of the country that has nothing at all to do with your original business. Buying cash flow with someone else's money is tantalizingly simple, and the steps that you take to do it are as straight as a Kansas highway.

A note of caution. Be sure you understand the laws surrounding Chapter XI and the risk of signing personal guarantees. You might match the achievements of Bill Tauscher or of Bruce Engel by using the bankruptcy laws and personal guarantees for leverage; these tools may come in handy, enabling you to move swiftly to save your core company, but keep a smart attorney at your side when you wade into the areas of bankruptcy buy-outs and personal guarantees.

Chapter Five

Begin a Development Project

"Nothing propinks like propinquity," wrote Ian Fleming. And propinquity (or nearness) to cash is what the manager wants in tough times. Raising cash by effecting buy-outs, selling assets, and finding off-balance sheet assets is fine. But a faster means of raising cash is by "selling smoke"—by that I mean raising money by selling an idea, a conception of what the future might be, a project, a research and development (R&D) proposal, a job development proposal, a joint venture, or a spin-off right to something that does not yet exist. Think I may be smoking something? You are wrong. Hollywood, a $9 billion industry (U.S. box office receipts plus home video) has been doing it for sixty years.

Independent movie producers sell smoke so well, there should be an Oscar for "maximizing leverage for a feature film." Beginning with only a script, they raise millions of dollars of other people's money to produce a movie. They start by signing the "sizzle"—a "name" actor or director. The premise is the same in other businesses. Find the sizzle in your company and write a business plan for it. Here are some of the ways to raise cash from the sizzle.

GRANTS TO DISPEL THE DARKNESS

If you or your company has a development project that has not been worked on for quite a while, it is time to haul it out and dust it off.

R&D Grants

There are numerous sources of R&D grants, the most plentiful of which are the eleven states that have grant programs ranging from $100,000 to $500,000. In certain cases, you do not have to relocate your company to the states that offer the grants in order to receive them. ScanTech Corporation in Santa Fe, New Mexico, has raised $350,000 in Ohio and $150,000 in Pennsylvania to develop the company's digital X-ray imaging products. Here is how it works.

ScanTech's product is a system that combines X-ray and computer technologies to allow on-the-spot digital imaging that, unlike X-ray film, can be highlighted and manipulated to suit the viewer's needs. ScanTech has tested and is considering a wide variety of applications for its system. A Pittsburgh hospital is checking out the system for use in chest X-rays. General Electric is looking at using it to examine aircraft turbine blades. Through a joint program with Ohio State University, ScanTech continues to explore welding applications on different metals. Using a grant from the Department of Energy, the company's president is working at a Los Alamos laboratory to see whether linear accelerator technology can be used in ScanTech's system to accelerate electrons for X-ray generation. The system's use for airport security is also under study.

The company's founder, Everett Ellin, learned fund-raising techniques while assistant director of the Guggenheim Museum, and he has raised nearly as much in state grant funds—$500,000—as he has in venture capital from private investors.

Alas, you protest, grants take too long to get, and they are uncertain sources of capital. Not at all. The eleven states that provide R&D grants cite ten and one-half to fifteen weeks for processing and funding a grant application. For information on how to raise grant money, contact the economic development directors in each state. The repayments are hardly odious. New Mexico charges 2 percent of the sales of the product developed with its funds for a period of eight years from the date of the grant. That is the equivalent of a non-interest-bearing, eight-year, participating, unsecured loan. Most of the states that offer grants permit the company to add some portion of the financing for management services, consultants, and travel. The eleven states that offer R&D grants are listed in Table 5.1.

The point of raising R&D grant funds when your company is out of cash and in a survival mode is to develop a salable product, one that will generate future profits. Further, you can pay the salaries of two to five of the company's senior engineers or scientists. You can demonstrate to your bank that the company's viability is as strong as tempered steel and that if the bank pulls the plug on the company before the new development project is completed, it may be one of banking's darkest days. Finally, you can cheer the rest of the staff, particularly the hardy crew that is negotiating a stretch-out plan with 350 fiery-eyed creditors (whose strategy is described in Chapter 11). By actively pursuing an R&D program, you dispel the darkness.

If the R&D team produces a prototype with the grant funds, and if the prototype works in its alpha test, the company will still require capital to build production models for beta tests, for sale or licensing purposes, or to attract expansion capital.

Table 5.1   States Offering Grants

State	Grant Amount
Connecticut	$300,000
Illinois	100,000
Indiana	100,000
Michigan	250,000
Mississippi	100,000
New Jersey	150,000
New Mexico	500,000
North Carolina	50,000
Ohio	350,000
Pennsylvania	35,000
Rhode Island	100,000

Many of the states that offer grants also offer long-term, low-interest-rate loans.* Ohio offers the 166 Program, which provides working capital to companies that locate manufacturing facilities in Ohio; amounts up to $1.6 million are offered over fifteen years at an interest rate of 6 percent per annum. To that, you can add appropriate federal grant money. The Urban Development Action Grant (UDAG) provides up to 33 percent of the total project cost via a grant to the community, which in turn loans it to the company at interest rates as low as 4 percent per annum. A Community Block Development Grant (CBDG) provides up to $350,000 of the total project cost along the same lines. The local director of the state's economic development agency can help your company apply for a UDAG or a CBDG. Although these grants take a few months to generate funds, they are available in every state to applicants who develop or expand a business in any HUD-qualified area. Such an area is defined by the age of its buildings and the absence of new development for many years. Two areas that are HUD qualified are the South Bronx and, because of its large number of old houses and buildings, Beverly Hills, California.

If your company is at least 51 percent owned by Vietnam veterans, you can move to the head of the line for a Small Business Administration (SBA) 504 loan, or an SBA loan guarantee to purchase equipment or component parts or to have additional working capital. The SBA, which typically guarantees 90 percent of bank loans (up to $550,000 repayable over eighty-four months), will stretch to $1 million if your company produces goods for export. Most small business owners can receive SBA assistance, but if you served in Viet Nam, you will receive priority treatment. The SBA generally requires hard collateral and personal guarantees.

Let's look at several creative ways to use these direct loan and loan guarantee programs. If your company sells franchises or dealerships, you can assist your clients in obtaining financing to build out, equip, and purchase inventory for their locations. Are you in the business of selling and installing equipment to small and medium-sized customers? To accelerate sales, take

---

* For details, see another of my books: *Upfront Financing* (New York: John Wiley & Sons), 1988.

your customers to their local economic development agency and work on a loan or lease guarantee program. If you are in real estate development or construction, the UDAG and CBDG programs are hog heaven. You can rebuild and renovate downtown America with these programs; then you can rent the renovated buildings out to quality tenants. For the street-level shops, purchase franchises of some of the best retail concepts; then finance your start-up costs with SBA loan guarantees. You can find able people to run the shops, and the franchising companies offer training in pizza throwing, ice cream serving, and store layout. Using a multiplicity of grants, loans, and loan guarantees, you can buy, renovate, and develop beautiful old buildings in many downtown areas. In this manner, the waterfront area in Portland, Maine, bounced back ten years ago.

The state of Oregon offers grants up to $250,000 for businesses that will operate on its waterfront. The state of Illinois will pop $100,000 into early stage companies with an innovative new product. There are twenty-seven states with innovative financing programs. The balance of the states have offices that promote federal programs. Snatch your company from the jaws of disaster by packaging your development program, visiting the nearest economic development office, and finding out how to spin gold out of straw.

Foundation Grants

There are thousands of grants available from foundations established through entrepreneurial wealth from a previous generation—Kellogg, Carnegie, Ford, and others. Robert Maxwell, the English tycoon, recently created a foundation to invest his publishing fortune in new forms of medicine. Recently, U.S. West announced that $20 million will be set aside for grants in its regional market. Entrepreneurs in service industries can obtain grants up to $500,000 to study problems that affect various aspects of society. The Kellogg Foundation provides grants for studies involving senior citizens. Park Communications provides grants in those small towns in which it publishes newspapers. The Sam Walton Foundation provides grants in small towns in which it operates stores.

A list of foundations can be found in any major library. Assign one of your less-overworked secretaries to contact the foundations in order to determine their areas of interest. Then, approach them with your development project.

R&D LIMITED PARTNERSHIPS

If movies can be marketed via box office as well as home video, your development package can be marketed in two arenas as well. For example, with the same business plan you use to pursue a grant from a state funding source, you can go after funding from an R&D Limited Partnership (RDLP) as well. There are two major RDLPs in the country, one of which is managed by R&D Funding Corporation, a division of Prudential-Bache Securities in Sunnyvale, California, and one of which is managed by Merrill Lynch Research & Development Fund, L.P., in New York. These two funds have more than $300 million in aggregate capitalization, and their minimum investment is $1 million, with an emphasis on larger amounts.

R&D Funding Corporation and Merrill Lynch spend considerable time investigating the patents, the market need, the competition, and the capabilities of the scientists and of the management team that will attempt to commercialize the product whose development they are funding (due diligence). Irving Weiman, a senior official of R&D Funding Corporation (with whom I have worked closely on an $8.3 million funding) says, "We have to go beyond the normal due diligence that a venture capital fund would do because we take one more risk than they do: the development risk." As a result, to receive a commitment from R&D Funding Corporation or from Merrill Lynch, you must have a solid story to tell—that is, you must have a qualified management team, a large market need, weak competition, a less expensive but more efficient product, an enlightened marketing strategy, and an alert and helpful board of advisors. In addition, you will have to expect a four- to six-month due diligence process.

Investment banking firms that do not have their own RDLPs are capable of privately placing $1 million or more in your RDLP. However, their methods are more rigid; they will perform lengthy due diligence, and they will take time to prepare a private placement memorandum. Furthermore, your company may be required to pay the investment bank's out-of-pocket expenses and legal fees if the financing aborts. And even if the investment bank gives your company a commitment letter, it is no better than a commitment to make their best effort. There are, however, success stories. Centocor successfully raised $4 million via an RDLP through F. Eberstadt & Company in 1985, and in addition to some tax shelter features, investors received low-priced warrants to buy Centocor's common stock, which has tripled since the RDLP financing closed. The funds were used for research into oncogene therapy for certain kinds of cancer, and investors are considerably ahead on their 1985 investment.

If you have contacts with many wealthy people, your company can self-underwrite an RDLP, thereby saving the investment bank costs. You will have to stand the legal fees, which are not small, but you probably did most of the hard work when you wrote the grant application, so that the lawyer's task is to make it viable as an offering circular. Tell your lawyer to protect you from securities fraud but not to rewrite the business section of the RDLP offering. Borrow a handful of prospectuses from a local stock brokerage office in order to learn the layout and the information requirements of an offering circular.

RDLPs provide that the technology and the know-how that the limited partners pay for become their property; the limited partners take title to it. Your company may enter into a license agreement with the RDLP to "make, use, and sell" the product for the RDLP at such time as a product is indeed developed. But, the limited partners are informed in the prospectus that "there can be no assurance that it will." This lack of assurance places the limited partners at risk. And, being at risk, they can write off the losses incurred on research and development against their passive income (interest, rents, and other license fees). Also, certain states provide a deduction against state income taxes for investors in RDLPs.

The prospectus states the amount of license fees the limited partners will receive at varying sales levels of the product. For example, 10 percent of sales up to $50 million, 5 percent from $50 million to $100 million, and 2 percent thereafter for a total of twelve years. Note that RDLPs have time limits. They also have general partners who manage the development and who receive a none-too-generous annual management fee—that is, 3 to 5 percent of the amount raised per annum. This fee adds to your company's working capital.

THE ROLL-UP

If the product that the RDLP develops does in fact become a blockbuster success, the 10-percent fee on product sales (owed to the limited partner investors) may become too large in terms of your company's ability to raise additional financing. For example, assume that the size of the RDLP is $5 million, that your company has earnings of $1 million after taxes, and that two million shares of common stock are outstanding. If the blockbuster product has estimated sales of $10 million per annum, your company will be paying the RDLP $1 million per annum. Then, if your company requires additional financing, the new investors are likely to protest shipping $1 million per annum to the RDLP group when it could double the earnings and double the value of the stock. At this point, your investment bankers would doubtless advise you to effect a roll-up— that is, thank the limited partners for their financial assistance and get rid of the RDLP by exchanging shares of your company's common stock for limited partnership interests.

Roll-ups are a novelty in the financial community because RDLPs are a 5-year-old phenomenon, and some positive successes are just now being harvested. Genentech rolled up two of its limited partnerships of $150 million in 1987 by giving away nearly 40 percent of its common stock. It seemed a fair exchange, and the Genentech limited partners did not complain. On the other hand, Forbes recently reported that two real estate limited partnerships that were rolled up gave the partners 10 percent of the amount of their investment with little or no prospect for future upside potential. Remarkably the partners took the roll-up lying down.

THE LITIGATION GAME

Thomas L. Kelly, Jr., is the founder of TIE/communications in Stamford, Connecticut, and while assisting TIE to raise capital in 1976, I learned enough survival strategies from Kelly to last a lifetime. At the time, Kelly was battling AT&T for the right to interconnect TIE's brand of telephone with AT&T's lines. Kelly had to traverse a tunnel of crises that was longer and darker than that of any other manager I have worked with; every time Kelly gained a foot, AT&T piled more boulders in his path. It was hard enough just convincing customers to purchase TIE's telephones rather than rent AT&T's; the question of service and reliability was a real problem. Could a customer count on TIE to service the telephones if they broke?

Not only did Kelly and his chief operating officer, Leonard Fassler, push through a $350,000 R&D grant with the state of Connecticut—no mean feat when you are an importer/assembler without a product development division—but Kelly treated TIE's adversarial situations as development projects. He was one of the first managers to "sell" litigation to investors. Kelly treated his lawsuits from AT&T and his lawsuits against AT&T as if they were assets he could pledge. He convinced both investors and lenders that TIE would eventually win huge settlements. As a result, attorneys agreed to work on a contingency basis; investors bought off on the business plan, regarding possible litigation wins as additional capital gains or downside protection; and the financially astute venture capital partners of Allen & Company invested $300,000 in TIE after the company nailed down its R&D grant.

Others have carried litigation to a higher level by selling interests to pay legal fees. For 30 years, Dr. Glenn Gould fought his claim to the invention of the laser with capital provided in part by Eugene Lang's Refac Technology Corporation. In 1987,

Gould was awarded the victory, which is expected to result in over $30 million in royalties by 1990. Refac, an American Stock Exchange Company, should receive close to $5 million.

Certain litigation wins, such as antitrust awards, provide treble damages to the winner. If two or three large suppliers stop shipments to you at the same time and effectively shut your company down, it is conceivable that they colluded. If not, why did each supplier stop shipping the same week? You may have an antitrust cause of action against them. A litigation attorney might be willing to take your company's case on a contingency basis—that is, payment of his expenses plus one-third of the win—or if not, you might sell interests in your litigation in order to pay the legal bills.

As one who has brought litigation against large corporations, it is clear to me that small companies can beat the giants at the litigation game. The reason is simple. The big guys do not work as hard at it. It is necessary to move quickly in litigation, but big corporations are scared—afraid that their image will suffer from having wronged a little guy.

I am not making a case for harassment lawsuits. Rather, if your company has been damaged and can point to the damages, add them up and show the flow of events that caused them; then, by all means, enter the litigation game as if it were a development project. A vigorous prosecution by an eager beaver lawyer can get you a win and can enable your company to raise money by leveraging the litigation.

THE ANNOUNCEMENT EFFECT

Public relations, or PR, is a curious art. We are all familiar with the adage, "If your actions speak loudly, then you do not have to talk about them." But in a cash crunch, you have to bear in mind that the folks in the trenches are getting bashed by the creditors and need material to hand out. They need a new story to tell the collection agencies and the in-house collectors—something to get their hopes up.

Therefore, when you are awarded the grant, or when you file the $16 million lawsuit, telephone the local newspaper and get a story written about the event. Then you can give copies of the article to the accounts payable team to send to certain creditors (not the ones you are suing). Be sure your banker gets a copy as well. He will need it for the file—to show the examiners as well as his loan committee.

Public relations can cut both ways. While you are entrenched in your work-out plan, invisibility is your friend. The trade press can crucify you. Do not forget who buys advertising space in the trade press: your creditors. Thus, any sign of financial trouble at your shop will be gleefully reported in the trade press. However, a good strategic move would be to send a photostat of the litigation article to the newspapers that are near the headquarters of the big corporation you are suing. Let them get a call from their nervous banker about the $16 million lawsuit. It could send a dark cloud of concern over their otherwise bright day.

In litigation battles, he who does the most homework wins. Lawsuits are won or lost before anyone sets foot in court. Also, 80 percent of commercial lawsuits are settled out of court. Go through all your files involving the litigants very carefully. Ask staff members for their correspondence. Investigate the tiniest details. Follow the slimmest leads. You may find that the supplier that cut you off was supposed to give thirty days' notice. You may find incidents of defective merchandise. There may be inconsistencies in performance. You might find a possible conspiratorial trail.

A large corporation sued one of my clients, but the department head who brought the suit had submitted his resume to my client eighteen months previously. He had also requested personal gifts and favors. These items were dug out of the file, and copies were sent to the company. The employee was terminated immediately, and the suit was dropped because the employee would have been unable to stand up to cross-examination. If the correspondence file, the shipment file, and the payables files had not been searched page by page, such an Achilles' heel would never have been found.

SUMMARY

In the pit of economic doom and gloom, pull your best innovative idea out of moth balls, dust it off, bring it up to date, and run it over to your state's economic development office. Find out whether your package is do-able in your state—one of the forward-thinking twenty-seven—or if not, check the federal funding programs that are available. You may be able to pull together five or six layers of funding without reaching for your own billfold. The states are competing for jobs; take advantage of it. The best time is when it looks as though the bottom has dropped.

Do not stop with state and federal funding programs. Use the package to attract R&D funds via RDLPs. You can approach the master limited partnerships that operate like venture capital funds or the investment banking firms, or you can sell your own RDLP with the aid of an experienced attorney. If your innovation hits pay dirt by becoming an important new product, you may have to roll up the RDLP later on.

Talk about your good news when you receive funding. Clip articles and let your accounts payable clerks tell your worried creditors about the news. Let them know that your company is valid, innovative, and doing important things. The development projects may not be paying the bills, but they show strong forward momentum. Public relations can be a powerful weapon; people remember the stories they read about you although they cannot remember where they read them. An article in your hometown newspaper should be clipped, photostated, and mailed to the company's key vendors—it should be used strategically as part of the company's overall redirect-and-grow plan.

Funding a litigation and funding a development project have much in common: you can leverage or sell interests in both; both require preparing a written plan, doing lots of homework, doing a lot of strategic thinking, and using public relations carefully. Both require selling your vision of a future event to others then reselling it in other markets to maximize your cash flow from a single event. When things look the grimmest, the time is best to go out and develop something.

Chapter Six

Involve More People

While producing a biblical movie, the colorful director Samuel Goldwyn was heard to yell at his staff: "Why only twelve disciples? Go out and get thousands." You too should think big—involve lots of people. Bring in people who will have a stake in your success or failure, who will catch cold if you sneeze, who will go down with you if you go down.

LAY OFF THE RISK

During hard times, most people develop a bunker mentality. But not you. You will reach out to the community to involve others in the success or failure of your company. Make them responsible for a portion of your success with the knowledge that they will profit handsomely from a happy ending. If you share the upside with key people in the community, they will move heaven and earth to help you succeed. If you operate in several communities, form regional boards of advisors. Implement this aspect of your survival plan meticulously and be clear in delegating responsibility and in establishing the rewards for success.

Movie producers seem to achieve people leverage better than others. Their objective is to get many people to assume a portion of the risk for the completion of the movie and to hold on to as much of the profit as they can. Take careful note of how the independent movie producer involves people. He juices them with points, cajoles them with the idea of being involved, and twists arms with pieces of the action. He uses, schmoozes, and bemuses people until they commit. Here's how it's done.

The independent movie producer obtains a sixty-day commitment from the star and the director to block out sixteen weeks sometime in the future. Now he has two key players at risk. They are leveraged. Next he asks the television network to advance a portion of the movie's budget for the rights to air the movie at a certain date in the future. The network will put up a letter of credit subject to a performance bond. The performance bond requires that the director create a budget. He agrees to do so if paid $60,000 for his time. The network is leveraged subject to the producer raising $60,000, which is made easier by the producer having the commitments of three players—the star, the director, and the network—and so it goes. Were the movie to unravel, these three players would have to redo their plans, budgets, and cash flow projections. The producer scampers around getting dozens of people committed for "dates certain" and for fees or payments; this creates a great deal of forward momentum.

In the field of movies, every player—except the distribution companies, lenders, and networks—is an agent, an entrepreneur if you will, living from deal to deal. When they commit their services to a block of time in the future, it becomes expensive and painful to adjust those plans. The players have a vested interest in the movie being made. Thus, they begin to assist the producer by widening his circle of contacts in order to assure that the movie is made.

You can transfer this people-leveraging strategy to your company and use it as a means of generating cash for a project, expansion, buy-out, or real estate development. The key players to contact are all those in the community who stand to benefit if your company pulls off its plan. Include *all* of those people, government agencies, and entities who stand to benefit.

Begin with the region's *economic development director.* This person's job is to fill area plants with workers. He may have his heart set on a political career, and that will be made more realizable if he puts people to work. The economic development director will tell you what is available in the way of state funding, job-training aid, federal funding, tax incentives, and other economic assistance programs. But at the least, pick the director's brain for contacts—the names of helpful people, venture capital clubs, wealthy investors, and regional corporate pension funds.

A second important player is the president of the *electric utility company* in the region. Because more people will use more electricity, his corporation benefits if more jobs are created in his region. As a result, electric utility companies usually set aside a portion of their capital—frequently through their employee pension funds—for investing in innovative businesses in the region. Innovation means new solutions to problems that affect large numbers of people. Innovation builds strong companies and creates lots of jobs, and that translates into more electricity usage. Thus, attempt to gain the electric utility company's support for your innovative new product or project. Make them feel a part of it. In consideration for their gaining some credit for the project, they must assist you either with financing or with introductions to sources of financing.

Managers of *pension funds* in the region should be contacted as well in order to see whether they invest a portion of their capital in venture capital projects. Investment departments of commercial banks are also candidates because they frequently manage pension fund assets. Physician groups frequently have sizable pension funds, and if your project is medical in nature, it could interest them. You might consider offering a position on the board of advisors and additional stock options to the medical advisors for the investment.

Insurance companies are keenly interested in innovative investments, and practically all of them with assets in excess of $150 million have invested in venture capital funds or have made direct venture capital investments. Approximately 5 percent of an insurance company's assets may be invested in non-interest-bearing securities, under the rules of the state insurance commission. This 5 percent is known as the "basket," and it grows every year as the insurance company's assets grow. The trade-off to the insurance company, in addition to potential capital gain on its investment, is to insure the company's officers, plant, equipment, or other parts of the project. This is not a huge incentive to the insurance company, but if you involve the leading agent in the region and have him carry the ball for you to the investment committee, the premiums on your company's business will be very important to him. He will calculate the fee, convert it to the new boat he wants to buy, and push his company very hard for you.

Contact the various *suppliers* of equipment or inventory to the project. Fred Smith kicked off the $96 million financing for Federal Express Corporation by first going to his principal supplier, General Dynamics Corporation, from which Federal Express would purchase hundreds of Falcon jets. General Dynamics committed to a portion of the start-up financing. That level of commitment demonstrates a great deal of faith in the project to other players because the supplier is risking capital and providing extended shipping terms or credit.

The local *university* may surprise you with what it is capable of contributing. If your project is science-based, the university might agree to a joint venture with you and provide scientific assistance or laboratory space. The local university may manage a focus group test of a new product for you at no charge. If your company has several alumni among its employees, a visit to the university endowment fund in search of an investment could prove beneficial. Many universities invest in venture capital funds or make direct venture capital investments. Grinnell College invested in Intel Corporation at an early stage. Rochester University invested in Xerox Corporation when it was a seedling. Both universities now have multimillion dollar endowments as a result. In consideration for the university's investment, you could agree to provide a gift of future personal capital gains to the endowment fund. You might also agree to hire accountants from the business school.

Do not overlook the local *junior college* president. His task is to place graduates in jobs. If your project will require semiskilled workers, you can agree to hire his graduates in consideration for his assistance in endorsing your project, introducing you to sources of capital, and opening some doors that have been closed to you. Perhaps he is on the board of the local insurance company or electric utility. A call from him to the presidents of both corporations beats a cold call from you.

Who else stands to benefit? When William C. Norris founded Control Data Corporation in 1967, he did so with a self-underwritten public offering. He and Control Data's chief financial officer, Willis K. Drake, drank countless cups of coffee with potential investors at Mrs. Strandy's Coffee House in St. Paul, Minnesota. One day when stock sales went too slowly, Norris called on the chairman of 3M Corporation and painted a glowing picture—but to no avail. While the coffee shop investors became millionaires, the chairman of 3M Corporation had to settle for sour grapes.

Do not let the turndowns get you down. Raising money is a numbers game. You have to see five potential sources to get one investor. But when you do get a turndown, try to get the reasons for it. Learn from it. Some company presidents believe that a resounding "no" is the best propellant they could hope for. It makes them want to show the bastards how wrong they were. Bruce Engel, who brought WTD out of Chapter XI with a $500,000 personal guarantee, is propelled by fear rather than by turndowns. He told *Success!* magazine: "Live with fear and accomplish things that make you proud."*

Commercial bankers are risk averse, and unlikely to provide any form of upfront help. However, you can ask them what they might do and when they might do it, once the project has begun. For instance, perhaps the bank will commit to financing your accounts receivable from the beginning, before your company has positive net worth. Perhaps it will make an equipment loan, open credit card accounts, finance floor-plan inventory, provide you with a second mortgage, or assist key employees in buying stock via loans on their cars, houses, or boats. Be persuasive with several bankers, and try to leverage one into helping you lift off in return for becoming the company's depository.

* Bruce Engel, *Success!* (December 1987), pp. 54-56.

Consultants generally have excellent contacts, people who can get things done. "New York is a town where people are used to finding money," the saying goes. A New York street-wise consultant may be able to find the missing piece of the puzzle: the insurance firm that guarantees an equipment loan, the equity gap lender, the publicity wizard who can place your story in *The New York Times*, the barter company, and so forth. The small company manager should ask other companies to recommend consultants who have been helpful to them. Check the consultants' references. Establish explicit compensation packages for the consultants with the cash portion tied to performance. Be clear and obtain the consultants' commitment to your company.

OTHERS TO INVOLVE

Even after you have involved ten or so outside people and consultants, there are not enough key people working on cash. More people must be leveraged. The troubled company must put itself in a position where others will suffer if it fails. I once worked with a manager whose background was in public relations and who knew how to do this very well. The manager brought eight separate organizations and people together in a room and made each one responsible for a part of the company's financing, acquisition, or whatever was to be accomplished. She brought in the accountants to prepare the financial statement projections, and their payment was tied to a successful deal. The lawyers were leveraged in the same way. The local industrial development agency, who wanted to see jobs created in the region, was pushed to dig deeper into its pockets. The insurance agent, who might gain the key-man and any liability business if he found money, was pressured to find a loan or a creative form of financing. The stockbroker, who might get the right to underwrite the company's new issue, was asked to search through his Rolodex for names of investors. An agency of the federal government, which might guarantee loans, was leaned on. The commercial banker, who might finance part of the transaction and thus earn the deposits, was asked to dig deep, as was the commercial finance company officer, who might take another piece of the loan. She also invited a venture capitalist for the equity component. She then squeezed them together, served wine and a tasty meal, and catalyzed discussion to try to get a deal to happen. She shmoozed them, cajoled them, laughed with them, and kept serving the wine and food. Nobody could leave without knowing what his role was or when he was expected to return with a done deal. All of the professionals were working on a speculative basis, so if a deal did not happen, they would not get paid. To leverage the local government agencies, she effectively used the press to announce several hundred jobs to be created or saved, as the case might be. Then if the deal fell apart, their agencies would suffer the slings and arrows of public dismay, not she. When others are involved whose payment or reward depends upon something happening, something usually happens. The lady knew how to get the most out of people.

FORM OR STRENGTHEN YOUR BOARD OF DIRECTORS

The obvious place to find assistance is the company's board of directors. It is critical to put together a strong board of directors. These people should be experienced businessmen, not lawyers, not accountants, not bankers. You want board members who have lived through the downside, worked through crises, and survived in markets that had been given up for dead. Your candidates should also know how to scale up production; how to design and implement a marketing plan; how to locate, interview, hire, compensate, and manage middle managers; how to enter new markets; and how to terminate people without being sued. A responsive, intelligent board of directors can be attracted by getting them excited about your tenacity, wisdom, and competitiveness as well as the company's growth prospects. Do not forget to sell them a small amount of the company's common stock at a cheap price.

Do You Communicate Well?

Raising money requires good communications skills, speaking well. Frequently, managers have it all in their heads—the plan for survival, the growth, the ultimate success—but they cannot communicate it well enough to key people in or out of their company.

In business, communications from the top down are often extremely poor. The president has the corporate identity, the product designs, the marketing plan, the production plans, and the advertising plans in his or her head. The president means to sit down one day and tell his or her people the roles they are expected to play, but things keep cropping up that must be attended to. The company runs off like a loose flywheel, with predictable results. Sales of certain products fall, sales of others rise, personnel come, personnel go, some customers are satisfied, and others bring litigation against the company. The results are uneven, and productivity is less than it could be.

This kind of difficulty is normally part of a larger problem or series of problems. It is not unusual, in instances such as this, for the president to be replaced by a more seasoned manager in the role of chief executive officer. If (1) the commercial banker is being uncooperative, (2) the investors will not put in more capital, and (3) customers are complaining about service, a communications consultant may be able to locate the problem.

You might consider using a communications consultant to interview the key people in the company, making certain that they understand clearly what is expected of them and that they can do the job assigned to them. Of course, this process takes several days because a thorough interview frequently lasts an hour.

When the interviews are analyzed and synthesized by the consultant, they are presented to a committee of the board of directors. In many cases, more than half of the officers and managers of the company do not know the company's goals and objectives or their roles in achieving them. If they do, they lack definition, and they certainly do not know whether they are doing what is expected of them.

AVOID THE ODYSSEY

Unfortunately, there exists a class of people who would steal the gold coins off the eyes of dead Sicilians awaiting burial. These pariahs have the eyes of eagles, the sense of smell of buzzards, and the hunting instincts of hawks. When your company is gasping for lack of cash, they somehow find you and recommend the most preposterous odysseys for you to undertake in order to raise your capital.

One of their pathetic schemes is the "prime international bank guarantee." These *havrakiddushas*—that is Yiddish for people who prepare the body for burial—ask for a $25,000 fee upfront to obtain a guarantee for a bank loan (which you have to arrange), and the guarantor is a "prime international bank." There is no tooth fairy, and there is no prime international bank guarantee that your banker will loan against. You should thank the person who offered you this unique source of funding and suggest that if he will provide you the names of five of his happy clients, you will speak with them. He cannot provide this list, so the conversation ends there.

A second caller will offer you a $10 million loan from an insurance company to meet your $3 million requirement. You will receive the smaller number but repay the larger, thus providing a handsome return to the lender, $100,000 in monthly interest for $3 million at risk. The $7 million, less fees, is put into treasury bills. Unless your mother raised dumb children, this deal should be tossed away as well. Politely ask the caller for references of satisfied borrowers, and when he demurs (as he certainly will), thank him for the offer.

Know Your Lender! Never borrow money from unknown sources—such as "Arab loans"—because they may be people who chomp cigars and speak out of the corners of their mouths. Their collection policies include shooting off your grandmother's kneecaps and other forms of pressure. My rule of thumb: if I would not invite the lender to have dinner with my family, then I would rather pass up the loan.

While we are at it, there are one or two other useless characters to avoid. The public shell merchants prey on hapless companies that desperately need funding. They control public companies that have neither assets nor liabilities—this means no cash for you—but they will try to convince you to merge your private company into their public shell and pay them a fee for the trouble. Why would you fall for this? Because of the vanity argument.

The vanity argument is patently transparent. The shell merchant says, "Charlie, there are twenty million shares outstanding. After the merger, you will have sixteen million, the public will have two million, and I'll hold on to two million shares. We'll tell your story to a few brokers that control most of the public float, and the stock price will soar to one-eighth, or maybe one-quarter. Charlie, that'll make you worth $4 million. That's four large! You deserve wealth, man! You've earned it." Sweet music. Lovely lyrics. But plug your ears against the song of the sirens and heed them not.

SUMMARY

The point is this: when your company is wobbling on a fault line, involve intelligent people who can help you, and place them at risk so that if you go down, they suffer. Make contact with the key players in your community. Use facilitative attorneys and accountants. Avoid strange offers for capital and any offers that require commitment fees in advance. Think like an independent movie producer. Reject money from unknown sources.

Chapter Seven

Put On a Seminar

You may think I have lost my marbles. Here you are in the center of the biggest battle for survival that you have ever waged. Your company's controller is handling dozens of dunning calls every day. Production has run out of component parts and cannot ship product. Your vice president of sales cannot hold his people because they have no product to ship. The process server is coming in the door with armfuls of lawsuits every day. Your banker has given you fifteen days to pay off a loan that you have personally guaranteed. You have not had a positive telephone call in so long that when the telephone rings, you feel like heading home to pet your dog and get some affection. And now I'm suggesting that you put on a seminar.

Well, look at it this way. You have a good brain, and you are an excellent communicator. How else could you have built the company in the first place? So get your brain in gear, engage your mouth, bring some people together, and start "yackin' at 'em." Seminar selling is the most inexpensive means of getting a product to market. Seminars churn up ideas, information, customers, and options. You need all of these things. Let me show you how to make it work for you.

ASSOCIATIONS

Senator Frank R. Lautenberg was an extraordinarily resourceful manager when he was growing Automatic Data Processing (ADP) in the 1970s. Following a $6 million public offering in 1967, Lautenberg and I hit the acquisition trail in search of data processing service companies to acquire. But the pickings were slim, and the cost of the search was high. A trip to Kentucky was wasted, as was a flight to San Diego. Lautenberg said, "Let's bring the acquisition candidates to us. We'll form an association." Of this need to acquire was born the Association of Data Processing Service Organizations, or ADAPSO, whose purposes today include lobbying, setting standards, and providing information.

But at the first meeting of ADAPSO, Lautenberg talked about ADP's acquisition goals and then took his seat while others spoke. One by one, napkins were passed along the table to Lautenberg who politely unfolded them in his lap and read the messages. "We are for sale. Call me in room 240. Jim Smith," one napkin read. A second napkin had the seller's financial statement scribbled on it. A third napkin said, "We would like to talk to you about being acquired. Call Bill in room 118." Without leaving New Jersey, ADP's president found a dozen solid acquisition candidates and began a series of acquisitions that created one of the country's most profitable companies.

Does your industry or niche have an association? If it does, would the coming together of the key players once or twice a year present opportunities for you? Think about it. Perhaps you could learn about the depth of the recession in other regions. Are there opportunities for you to effect bankruptcy LBOs? To make cheap acquisitions? If you form the association, you might invite a jobber or barter person to speak and then tell him about your attractive but slow-moving inventory.

At the association's first meeting, you might announce the sale of a division, a product line, or your entire company. Why place ads in the trade journal or call in a merger and acquisition broker? Stand up at the conference and say that your company is for sale. Or, more politely, say that you would like to explore areas of mutual interest with similar companies in the hopes of developing a mutually rewarding relationship. The other attendees will get the meaning.

Associations are not-for-profit industry groups whose stated mission is usually to support the members against hurtful legislation and to set standards of quality. Older associations made up of blue-veined, denture-breathed fossils of the industry attempt to block positive innovation. But new associations are fairly innocuous. The National Venture Capital Association speaks for all venture capital funds and tries to hold back increases in the capital gains tax rate. But the question is not what existing associations do or do not do; it is, what can you accomplish to generate cash by forming an association? The answer is probably, "plenty."

CLUBS

When I emigrated in 1981 from New York City to Santa Fe, New Mexico, one of the first things I did was to start a club. If one is to make a living servicing entrepreneurs, as I have chosen to, then one needs to see entrepreneurs. In the streets of New York City, if you shout, "Is there an entrepreneur in the crowd?" twenty people will come running. But in New Mexico in 1981, there were not many entrepreneurs to be found. New Mexico's economy is based on oil, farming, and tourism, with five federally funded scientific facilities and military installations.

The Venture Capital Club of New Mexico was founded as a forum for entrepreneurs to come together once a month and exchange ideas and meet investors, attorneys, accountants, and advertising consultants. At the same time, it could attract entrepreneurial companies that might catch my eye. In the last seven years, the Venture Capital Club of New Mexico has serviced over 2,500 entrepreneurs from all over the Southwest. I have also visited entrepreneurs in over twenty cities to help them launch clubs of their own.

The ideas flow a mile a minute once the entrepreneurs take the stage and give a three-minute presentation of their business plans. Numerous companies have raised capital through the club, and more important, the entrepreneurial process has become far better understood. Venture capitalists from New York and San Francisco have spoken at the club and left a few million dollars in New Mexico because they had a forum for considering an array of opportunities.

The club idea came to me as a result of adversity. I would not have initiated the Venture Capital Club of New Mexico if my deal flow had been large and continual in 1981. An investment banker cannot survive on marginal deals.

A manufacturer cannot survive with marginal customers, nor can a service company survive with marginal clients. The time when cash is short is the best time to start a club in order to bring customers or clients to you for a seminar. The object is to position yourself as the *giver* of information and assistance whether to people in the industry or to potential customers or clients who need information or assistance along with the product or service.

The wrong way to start a club is to invest in brick and mortar by constructing a facility such as the great white Info-Mart elephants in Boston, Atlanta, and Dallas. The right way to start a club is to be informal, nonthreatening, mobile, and laid back. People are unafraid to show their naiveté in informal settings. They are more likely to ask questions, exhibit their need for assistance, and tell you about their warts and all with a cocktail in their hand or while seated at dinner conference-room style.

Moreover, if your club becomes successful, your region will develop a reputation as a center of influence. People will come great distances to learn about it if the information flow is good. If you manufacture pet products, physical fitness equipment, or earth stations, you can initiate a monthly dinner club to bring producers, users, and fellow-travelers together. If you cannot meet the budget required for mailing announcements or for paying a speaker, ask one of the accounting firms to underwrite the club's budget. Accountants are the business community's great fishermen. They love nothing better than dropping their line in a pond of thirty to fifty business people.

It is important to have good speakers at a club meeting and to get the juices and vocal cords going. After the meal, ask everyone to stand at their place and give their name and a little information about themselves. You will find that people will stand and say, "I'm Phil Schultz, and I am here tonight to learn something about the subject." Having everyone stand and speak loosens the crowd and gets them in a chatty mood for the principal speakers.

You can expand a club into an association, trade organization, or a dues-paying organization that meets the needs of a large membership. It can be fluid and amoebalike in structure and capable of growth. Or it can be kept small while servicing purely regional needs. In either format, the club idea is a good way for you to generate customers, clients, publicity, awareness, new cash-generating ideas, and long-range product or service ideas.

TRADE SHOWS

The next level up from associations and clubs is the trade show. Whereas associations are not-for-profit information exchanges that help industry members make connections, trade shows are annual or semiannual bazaars where sellers display their products in endless rows of decorated booths and where buyers drop by and learn what is innovative, how it is priced, and when it will be on the market. Trade shows are working sessions for buyers and sellers alike. The Cannes Film Festival may be the most glamorous trade show, but all of the established industries have interesting ones. If the industry in which you are a manufacturer or of which you are a keen observer lacks a trade show, the door is wide open for you to launch one. The computer industry's trade show—COMDEX—was launched by an outsider in 1971, and it has grown too large to be accommodated by any single city's hotel beds; thus, there are now three COMDEX shows every year. The birth, growth, and development of the

COMDEX idea is worth spending a few minutes on. It may provide a clue to your company's salvation.

Sheldon Adelson, 54, found himself insolvent following the stock market slide of 1970. Since 1963 he had been a money finder and private investor in start-up companies that he then introduced to new issue underwriters for second-stage funding. But Adelson was illiquid and overextended in 1970 when the prices of stocks plummeted and the new-issue market dried up. "One day I woke up and found myself a million-and-a-half in the hole," Adelson told the authors of *The Computer Entrepreneurs.* *

His interests turned to condominium conversions, but he found an inexpensive magazine for sale. Adelson purchased *Communications User* magazine in 1972. He attended a condominium conversion trade show in 1972 and learned that the show's sponsor also published a magazine. An entrepreneur from the age of 16, Adelson immediately visualized trade shows as "living magazines," or "magazines in the flesh." In 1973, after changing the name of his magazine to *Data Communications User,* Adelson sponsored his first trade show, the Data Communications Interface show, where manufacturers of data processing equipment exhibited their products for end users. He learned the trade show business thoroughly over the next six years. In 1979, as the personal computer was emerging, Adelson saw the need for a trade show aimed at dealers and distributors. Eight months later, the idea for the first COMDEX (Adelson's dealer-oriented trade show) rolled out, and it has not stopped rolling since. In fact, computer industry trade shows that appeal to hobbyists and those that appeal to corporate data processing users have been left in COMDEX's dust.

Adelson's company, The Interface Group, has entered into facilities management contracts to operate trade shows in thirty other fields. The company has also founded other profitable spin-off businesses, such as offering tour operations, publishing the *COMDEX Show Daily* and other trade show newspapers, and exhibiting books and other materials that utilize

---

* Robert Levring, Michael Katz, and Milton Moskowitz, *The Computer Entrepreneurs* (New York: New American Library, 1984), p. 366.

Adelson's skills. The Interface Group's tour business is now the fifth largest in the United States. Adelson's empire includes over six hundred people and is believed to have revenues in excess of $200 million per annum.

A "living magazine!" What an exciting concept. If your industry has a magazine or newsletter, what about giving it a living magazine—a trade show. The revenue sources are as numerous as your imagination will permit:

1. Rent booth space
2. Sell ads in trade show daily newspapers
3. Sell or rent booth and exhibit materials
4. Buy a block of hotel rooms and resell them
5. Buy a block of airline seats and resell them
6. Buy a billboard space and resell it
7. Buy local television time and resell it
8. Buy a block of rental cars and rerent them
9. Tape and resell the proceedings to nonattendees
10. Publish the proceedings and resell them
11. Raise "official sponsor" money from consumer products companies
12. Provide services to the exhibitors—moving, storage, booth models
13. Rent attendee lists to others
14. Manage other trade shows under contract
15. Replicate the above revenue-generating facilities with trade shows that you manage.

The trade show must have a purpose. It is not enough just to want to hold an industry get-together in your community. The myriad film festivals that come and go around the country are living proof that trade shows require a broad purpose in order to be successful and lasting. If you are in the home video or audio cassette business, note that these two industries do not have trade shows. You could be the Sheldon Adelson of these markets. Trade shows require planning and some up front capital to attract exhibitors, but sponsors can normally be found among consumer products manufacturers and service organizations in exchange for their receiving appropriate consideration. Trade journals will provide you information about which industries lack trade shows. However, you should not stray far from your knowledge base.

SEMINARS

For service industries, particularly the newer ones, there is probably a need for a seminar. In fact, seminar-based marketing, initially brought to the American public by Weight Watchers International, is now part of the lexicon of entrepreneurial solution delivery methods. It is a legitimate marketing technique for services such as weight loss, new-age philosophies, entrepreneurship, investments, nutrition, a variety of psychotherapies, and health care. If you are a practitioner in one of these fields, why not consider promoting a seminar or a continuing series of seminars as a means of generating cash.

Jean Neditch, the founder of Weight Watchers International, developed several revenue-generating channels from seminar selling. Take-homes such as books, tapes, recipes, diaries, and the Weight Watchers' newsletter were placed at the back of the motel conference rooms. Why did H. J. Heinz eventually pay $60 million to Ms. Neditch for Weight Watchers International? Because Weight Watchers' name recognition was 91 percent—nine out of ten Americans recognized the name correctly—and that was nearly twice the percentage that recognized H. J. Heinz.

I can think of dozens of fields that do not have one well-known, magnetic person running its seminars. The field is wide open in

Family therapy	Direct-mail marketing
Company crisis management	Home business
Teenage chemical abuse	Franchise buying
Stress	Ways to clone Silicon Valley
Drugs in the school yard	Male sexual incompetence
Educational software	Air travel problems
Technology transfers	Medical malpractice

There are several keys to successful seminar selling, including easily reached locations, knowledgeable speakers, plenty of take-homes with strong logo identification, wide aisles that permit you to work the crowd, and long coffee breaks that give you the time to sell services to the attendees. Remember why you invited your customers to attend. You are looking for ideas from them about additional products or services that they need. Ask questions, such as: "What have you learned, Joe?" You might hear requests for more information on the different ways clients can earn money from your service—all of these are openings you can drive a truck through.

SUMMARY

You may be besieged by irate creditors, process servers at the door, and an ostensible crescendo of demands from managers proclaiming doom if you do not respond with cash instantaneously, but remain levelheaded. You have plans to jimmy the window behind your desk and let in a downpour of cash from a bizarre source: seminars.

You have discovered that your industry lacks a meeting place, a club, or an association. One of the reasons your creditors are uptight and downright mad is that they have poor information. That is a need—a demand curve in search of a solution—and you can fill it.

Call a meeting. Call it a trade group or an association, but call it in your city and invite customers and the press. Invite a good speaker, but leave time for long coffee breaks and post-seminar meetings in hotel coffee shops and bars. Let your customers discuss their problems. Form committees to study those issues, and put yourself on the committees. Plan to meet in three weeks, plan to discuss the gut issues, and plan to offer solutions. Maybe several customers fear a serious economic downturn. That is a leveraged buy-out opportunity.

Do not develop a bunker mentality—that is, do not crawl into a hole and pull a cover over you. Call for a seminar. Talk about the issues with those who want you to survive. Show some leadership. Be the captain of your destiny, not the boiler watcher.

LEARNING BACK-TO-THE-WALL STREET-FIGHT TACTICS

Chapter Eight

Change Banks

Hal Newman is a management consultant these days; he is not in books-on-cassette, an industry that he pioneered in the early 1980s with Newman Communications Corporation (NCC) in Albuquerque, New Mexico. A change in the lending policy at the company's bank drove the company into Chapter VII. Newman put his first equity financing together in my living room in 1982, raised additional money by taking a second mortgage on his house, and added to that with an initial public offering. By 1986, the company's sales had grown to $9 million, and its stock price had grown to $4 per share—a twenty-fold increase over the price that first-round investors paid. A second public offering was aborted at the last minute, and Newman sought to acquire Warner's Audio Tape Division to provide more cash flow and to double NCC's size to over $20 million.

Then NCC's primary lender was acquired by a large California bank that established a new policy: no loans to small companies outside of California. NCC had to begin repaying its loan, but it was unprepared because all energies had been focused on the acquisition, and the company was perilously illiquid. Cash could not be generated fast enough. The end came quickly, and the bank, being in a secured position, repaid itself with books-on-cassette.

In uncertain times, beware the commercial banking policy changes that can nail you to the wall. There are well over five thousand commercial banks in the United States, but there are less than one thousand competent commercial bankers—no offense intended. Competent commercial bankers either move up to bank management or move out to industry. A good loan officer does not remain in that job long. The banker who has always protected your account can leave, and you will become just a number at the bank.

How Banks Accidentally Kill Companies

Companies that maintain small depository relations suffer the most when banks overreact in economic hard times. Suddenly lines of credit are capped, overdrafts are not permitted, payroll checks are not cashed, and other evidences of bank fright come about without warning. Or in some cases, the company's banker leaves, and the new loan officer does not understand the company. Although the manager and the chief financial officer sit down with the new banker to explain their company, they are met with a stifled yawn.

What to Do at the New Bank

As part of your survival plan, change banks. Begin a larger depository relationship at the new bank. Pick an independent bank, and if possible a newly formed one. Take $200,000 of the new grant that you recently obtained and buy a certificate of deposit for ninety days. Then tell the bank's president that you want to borrow $100,000 for ninety days secured by the CD. When you repay it, you will have established an excellent credit rating with your new bank. Moreover, if it is a newly formed bank, you will have made the president a hero by opening a new account.

Read your local newspapers, looking for new bank formations and for the name of the new president. He needs to bring in new business accounts. Open a payroll account and a business account at the new bank while keeping a small balance and some activity at the old bank. Maintain an excellent relationship at the new bank, and if you must take risks, do that at the old bank where you are subject to less favorable treatment because you were a borrower or a client of a banker who may have been transferred or let go because of troubled loans.

If you travel out of town, you might open an account there as well. This will be your safety valve, a place to keep cash away from the sheriff if a lender or creditor gets a prejudgment attachment on your local bank accounts.

SURPRISE ATTACHMENTS

A prejudgment attachment can occur when a company owes a bank or a supplier a sum of money. The lender or supplier merely posts a bond for 100 percent of the amount owed in the county where the borrower has offices; then the lender makes an appointment with the United States District Court Judge and persuades him or her that the obligor is likely to flee the state with the assets or the money that belongs to the lender or creditor. The creditor's lawyer visits the judge ex parte—that is, without your lawyer present. Thus, you are a sitting duck for an attachment if you have been unable to pay an obligation for a period of time.

Apparently, once the creditor has the judge's signature on a writ of attachment, their lawyer is supposed to inform your lawyer that he has notified the sheriff or the U.S. marshall to begin removing your assets from your business and, if you are a general partner or a guarantor of the obligor, from your home. But it is my experience that some lawyers treat this convention with disdain.

Writs of attachment occur to unsuspecting borrowers; do not let that person be you. Be ready for a prejudgment attachment, and keep the bulk of your cash out of the county. But do nothing unusual that would create the suspicion that your company is transferring assets out of state in order to avoid the repayment obligation. The possibility of flight will lead to the attachment being sustained when you and the lender go head to head in court later on.

A DEFENSE AGAINST WRITS OF ATTACHMENT

Writs of attachment are increasingly popular with litigious attorneys and could become more so when the economy falters. If you think you may have to sword fight for your cash, *open an out-of-town bank account and keep most of your cash in it.*

It is impossible for you to know which creditor is over at the courthouse posting a bond and seeking a judge's signature. To avoid being put out of business by a creditor who is sweet-talking you with one side of his face while instructing his lawyer to get a writ of attachment with the other, follow these suggestions:

1. Open two operating accounts at banks located outside your county, and move funds by wire transfer as needed.
2. Deposit incoming checks into the account whose banker you "juiced" when he became president, and ask him to give you immediate credit in consideration for your maintaining a positive balance in a non-interest-bearing account.
3. Set up one day every two weeks on which you write checks for inventory, payroll, and general and adminis-trative expenses. On that day, wire the money from the safe bank to your local bank, then write your local checks—payroll and local vendors. But write your other vendor payments on one of the safe accounts. This keeps money in your county very briefly.
4. Document every out-of-state shipment of money and product with a supporting document to demonstrate to the court that you are not recklessly transferring assets out of state.

Fungible (nearly liquid) assets should be removed from your office or warehouse, to the greatest extent possible, and moved to the next county as well. Although this is an inconven-ience, it is prudent. Also, make photostats of all bookkeeping records and put the photostats in a safe place. An aggressive sheriff might elect to padlock your office door, and it will be useful to you to have a complete set of records, inventory, and cash in another county.

Although you can go into court and overturn a writ of attachment, the judicial process is slow, and it may be weeks before you get a hearing. By that time, your business could be on the meat rack.

SUMMARY JUDGMENT

A creditor who fails to make a writ of attachment stick will surely go back into court and attempt to obtain a motion for summary judgment. In this instance, you and your counsel are permitted to mount a defense and go into court to present your case. Your record keeping may save you. If it is a supplier that takes you into court, did you remember to document all of the returns for credit, all of the incomplete shipments, and other supplier errors that will make the court question the supplier's records? Perhaps the amount owing is incorrect.

If it is a bank or lender that hauls you into court, what about loan renewals? Do your records show that the loan is not overdue? Did the lender change its terms without informing you properly? Did the bank make some errors in handling your account, and did you notify the bank each time it made an error? Keep meticulous records in case you will someday need to show that your record keeping is impeccable.

WHAT BANKERS FEAR

Commercial bankers fear that they will not get repaid. They face loan committees, internal audits, and external audits by their CPA firms, by the Comptroller of the Currency (if they are national banks), and possibly by the FDIC. It is no wonder they become nervous when their loan to your company is overdue or when you miss an interest payment.

If your loan is fully collateralized, your banker will be less nervous about the possibility of your filing for protection under the Bankruptcy Act. A fully secured creditor cannot lose its collateral in a bankruptcy. A fungible asset, such as treasury bills or accounts receivable, provide the greatest comfort to the banker. But there is always the risk that the banker failed to file a Uniform Commercial Code evidence of collateral (UCC-1) properly or that someone else filed ahead of him. Your banker also fears that if your company goes into Chapter XI, his collateral may diminish in value and, in effect, put him in the position of an unsecured creditor.

As a result, he will work with you to the best of his ability to keep you solvent and out of bankruptcy. If you have a "clear the air" meeting with him, it is possible that he will advance you a new loan, tying up all of your assets; stretch the repayment on the new loan for six months, with interest due at the end; or take other steps to see you through tough times. The banker will probably agree to give you immediate credit on your customer deposits as well. However, if the sheriff comes to his branch with a court order to attach your accounts, there is nothing your banker can do to prevent the attachment. That is the reason to open new depository relationships while working with your current lender.

BELTS, SUSPENDERS, AND SAFETY PINS

Even if you succeed in leveraging your present banker and in opening an operating account in the next county, you are only holding up your pants with a belt and suspenders; you still need to pin the pants to your undershirt.

Policies change. Loan officers can leave and they are frequently sent to other branches. Loans can be suddenly called. Although one banker gave you immediate credit, a new one might insist on a seven-day hold on all deposits. This could be the death knell if it should happen at an inopportune moment.

That is why you need a third banker, one who works for an independent bank. Take him or her to lunch, explain your company, and open another operating account with a depository relation. Obtain a new credit card, and keep it relatively unused in case of emergencies. It may seem overcautious, but these are troubled times, and in troubled times, cash is king.

WHEN TO BLAME YOUR BANKER

In May 1985, Contempo International, a California clothes manufacturer, was forced into bankruptcy by its creditors. But Mal Sigman, Contempo's chief executive, refused to expire quietly. He decided that by failing to lend him the needed money, Wells Fargo created the cash crunch that caused his firm's demise. So Sigman got himself a lawyer and sued the bank for $140 million—several times more than the firm was ever worth.

Sigman is but one of a growing number of financially troubled businessmen to take advantage of so-called lender liability—a new brand of lawsuit in which businessmen sue their bankers. For the businessman, lender liability means one last chance to recoup losses. For the banker, it means that when a loan is called, a lender must not only worry about whether the borrower has the funds to pay but also worry about whether the borrower might sue him for asking for his money back. "[Lender liability] is becoming one of the hottest new areas of commercial litigation," says Barry Cappello, the California-based lawyer representing Contempo. "I turn down nine out of ten calls I get—I only take the absolute nightmares."

Another case of bank heavy-handedness arose in 1985 in the Sixth Circuit Court of Appeals in Ohio. The case pitted a wholesale grocer, KMC Company, against Irving Trust. Irving had refused to grant KMC an $800,000 loan, to which the grocer was entitled under a $3.5 million credit agreement. Without the financing, KMC was forced out of business. But before it expired, it sued, eventually collecting $8.3 million in damages on the grounds that the bank had acted in bad faith. Explains Helen Chaitman, an attorney with Wilentz, Goldman & Spitzer: "In effect, the judge said it was all right for the bank to terminate the company's line of credit, but not without notice.

The courts now say there is an inequity of bargaining power between a bank and its borrowers. And they mean to insure the banks deal with the little guy fairly."*

SUMMARY

Look for a new bank opening outside your county, and telephone the bank's president for an appointment. Make a substantial deposit in a ninety-day CD then borrow half the deposit and repay the loan in ninety days. You have done your banker a favor, and he owes you one. Ask him for immediate credit on all deposits; you'll get it. Treat that banker like a king; you may need another loan, or you may need a fast certified check to give to the sheriff someday.

How swiftly can things unravel for you? In as little time as it takes a creditor to go into court and get a writ of attachment on your bank accounts. If this happens, document the damage meticulously. At the same time, minimize the damage by maintaining out-of-county accounts. You can overturn a writ of attachment by showing that your company is not a candidate for flight. You can then win a large countersuit by carefully documenting the damage done to your company by the writ. Thus, from the jaws of defeat, you can kick ass and win a large jury award.

* Lisa Gubernick, "Lender Beware," *Forbes* (June 30, 1986), p. 106.

Chapter Nine

Leverage Your Customers

Who wants you to survive almost as much as you do? Your customers (or your clients, if you are in the service business). Customers are sometimes one-shot and almost always impersonal purchasers of your goods or services. Clients are repeat, personalized purchasers of your services. Commercial banks have customers, whereas investment bankers have clients. Clients would suffer over your demise longer than customers would, because their relationship with you is more intense. Both would miss you, and both need you to stay in business. They can be leveraged to squeeze out cash.

BE THE FIRST TO GET PAID

Never be lax in your collection policies. Establish a pattern of being paid first. We all know the three most important bills to pay: payroll, telephone, and withholding taxes. Make your company number four to get paid. You can do this with clarity upfront and with frequent reminders that you expect to be paid. If the customer or client slips a day or two beyond the day that payment is due, telephone the slow payer. If this is ineffective, send a telegram or fax a reminder notice.

Then, when your company gets into a cash crunch, change collection policies. Offer a 3-percent discount for payment in ten days. If you already do this, raise the discount to 5 percent.

Visit your slow-paying clients. Ask for the check. If you don't, somebody else will. If you are regarded as a company that will wait to be paid, you will always wait to be paid. This is not where you want to be in tough times.

NEVER BELIEVE FAIRY TALES

Two of the biggest lies in the world are "I'm from the government, and I'm here to help you," and "Your check is in the mail." When you hear the customer say this, ask him to put the check into an overnight courier envelope, provide your account number, and ask that the check be sent overnight. Don't stop there. Ask the customer to read you the airbill number so that you can trace it if it goes astray. In fact, you want to make certain that the check is being couriered. If you are worried that the check will not be sent by courier, ask the customer to wire it to your safe bank. Give him precise wire instructions and ask him to read them back to you. If you are making the customer pay $10 to send the wire, offer to knock $10 off the next invoice.

Use excuses to get payment accelerated. Tell the customer that you need it because the auditors are inside your company and because you want to show higher month-end sales. Tell the customer that a loan is coming due. Tell him that your job may be at stake or that an important payment date looms nigh. Get the cash before they crash.

SHORT-TERM CASH RAISING TECHNIQUES

The manager of a computer software company in Woodland Hills, California, purchased from his employer a division that produced software packages for truck dealers. The manager had agreed to a down payment of $120,000 and eight quarterly payments of $60,000 plus interest at 10 percent. Although the first $120,000 was paid in a timely manner, the first $60,000 was due in one day, and the manager had no means of paying for it.

The manager flew to the headquarters of a large truck dealer who had just recently placed an order and explained that in order for the client to have his product shipped, installed, and serviced, he would have to pay in advance. Because he had recently been sold on the idea, the truck dealer was on a high, anticipating what the product was going to do for him. He willingly paid the balance of nearly $90,000, and the entrepreneur made his payment in a timely fashion.

The best means of raising cash is to visit the customer to pick up the check. Once in his office, explain to the customer that you have been using all available capital for product upgrades and improvements and that you have temporarily depleted your bank account. He will benefit from these upgrades. Would the customer mind paying today rather than in thirty days? If so, you would be pleased to offer a 5-percent discount.

The stories told to me (in gales of laughter) about emergency cash-collection tactics that were thought up by entrepreneurs while standing on one foot in the customer's office would fill a book twice this size. I will try to abbreviate without losing the essence of each story. Suffice it to say that all of the stories begin with the manager on the road. He telephones his office from an airport pay phone and learns that either (a) payroll cannot be met, (b) an expected large check did not arrive, (c) the bank is putting a five-day hold on the company's deposits, or (d) all of the above. The manager hangs up and changes his plans. He cannot go back to the office tomorrow without a certified check in his pocket or a sizable wire transfer.

The manager checks his official airline guide, books a flight to the city where the heavily indebted customer is located, and appears there the next morning with ten creative stories that will explain why he is there and why he needs a check or wire transfer. The door opens, our hero walks in, and he immediately forgets his prepared stories. What pops out of his mouth could be any of the following:

You are very important: "Charlie, good to see you. Say, we have just divided our markets into five regions with customers in each region assigned to one person. Your region was picked by me because you are very important to our company. In fact, I will be personally servicing your account. That includes collecting payment for services."

We need your advice: "Jeff, how good it is to see you in your office. I have popped in on you to get your help. We need your advice. In fact, we would like you to head an advisory board made up of key customers that will provide product input, suggestions, ideas, and advice. What do you say, Jeff? Will you do it? Great, now if I could just see your controller while I'm here, it will be a banner day for me."

We need your advice and your time: "Bruce, how good it is to see you. Tell you why I'm in town. We're organizing a board of advisors to meet once a year, in the winter, in Jamaica, for golf and tennis, and to have you tell us more about our product. We want to hear from our best customers the ways that we can improve our product. Can you fit us in, Bruce, say mid-February, for a long weekend? We'll pick up the tab. That's terrific. I'll send you details when I get back to the office in a week. Say, Bruce, if you wouldn't mind pointing out the controller to me, it would save my office a call."

We need your advice and your time, and we want to score hero points: All of the above, but after the sentence about the weekend in Jamaica, add: "with wives."

We are in search of excellence: "Mary, nice of you to let me pop in this way. It is MBWA day for me—management by walking around—except I am flying around. I would like to interview the folks who are using our product in order to learn from them what they like, what they don't like, how we can do a better job, and, you know, things that good companies do to become even better. Will that interrupt anything, Mary? Good, then if you'll just introduce me. Oh, by the way, I would like to meet your controller and introduce myself, so we won't just be a bill that floats in every month or, in your case, twice a month—once with a collection notice."

My controller sent me: This is a coward's insert into one of the above conversations. One variation: "By the way, my controller asked me to pick up a check." A more subtle version: "My controller said that if I was in your neighborhood to pick up a check." The most cowardly of all: "My controller is a mean dude. He'll probably stomp my brains out if I don't come back with a check."

SELL SUBSCRIPTIONS TO YOUR SERVICES

The idea of receiving cash today for a service that may (or may not) be provided later dates back to the fifteenth century when Dutch capitalists began insuring the trips of explorers. The insurance industry is continually entrepreneurial, always thinking of new risks to buy and old risks to drop. But through all of its tough times, the insurance industry gets paid upfront.

Notwithstanding the fantastic success of the insurance industry, very few entrepreneurs have adopted this unique method of generating upfront cash from the customer. The magazine and newspaper industries have copied the idea by selling subscriptions, but until Sol Price came along, the prepaid subscription was a cash-generating idea in search of innovations.

Sol Price practiced law for seventeen years and then quit to launch Fed-Mart Corporation, a mass merchandiser and supermarket chain. Price pioneered private label brands and the one-stop-shopping concept. In 1975 he sold Fed-Mart to a West German buyer who fired him. Fed-Mart subsequently failed without him.

In 1975 Price formed The Price Company with his son Robert and introduced the concept of selling to *members only*— people who prepaid for the privilege of buying at steep discounts. The Price Clubs are large warehouses located near interstate interchanges. Businesses or individuals with retail sales licenses may become wholesale members by paying an annual $25 membership fee; for an additional $10 per person, a wholesale member may designate two additional buyers. Group memberships are available to bank and savings and loan employees, state and local government employees, certain utility and transportation workers, certain savings and loan customers, certain hospital workers, civilian federal employees, and members of certain credit unions. Just as prepaid health maintenance is becoming the tollgate in the health-care market, prepaid consumer buying is beginning to play a role in the consumer products market.

There are presently over 400,000 active wholesale members and some 4 million group members. The forty Price warehouses are each 100,000 square feet and open seven days per week. The company does not advertise; marketing is word-of-mouth. The company sales are derived from appliances (20 percent); food (22 percent); and hardgoods, liquor, softgoods, and sundries (28 percent).

At 71, Price is an astute marketer trained in the law, a field in which many of the best practitioners are subtle but excellent salespersons. Price raised his equity not from investors but from customers—or, if you prefer, from subscribers. With subscription dollars in the bank, Price can finance the build-out with long-term loans. The Price Club has been replicated by other general merchandise discounters, but not nearly as well. The market value of The Price Company is over $1 billion, and it reached that peak in under ten years.

The legal profession is beginning to use the prepaid subscription method to generate upfront cash tied to a new service: prepaid legal services. Jacoby & Meyers, who brought legal services to the common man via storefront locations, is leading the footrace to sign up groups for prepaid legal services. What a good idea to counter the tornado of litigation in our society: nip the rising cost of legal fees by paying upfront for a lawyer who agrees to cap his or her fees.

Fifteen years after its launch, Jacoby & Meyers has over two hundred offices and serves over 250,000 clients a year. Jacoby & Meyers manages the expanding enterprise within an entrepreneurship-type structure. Offices are managed by attorneys who are entrepreneurial and who make an upfront investment. The managing attorney of an office does not have a guaranteed salary; rather each is compensated for the profitability of the office. That gives each managing attorney the total management experience and allows each to become a responsive businessperson. The company's senior managers, in the meantime, sell the prepaid service to groups, unions, employees, and others, and the upfront payments mitigate the company's continual need for expansion capital.

With the prepaid subscriptions beginning to seep into areas of need, such as legal fees, the format is pretty well understood. A company could use it for all of the following new business areas:

Sporting goods
Drugs, health, and beauty aids
Home furnishings
Hardware and home improvement
Public relations services
Health care
Malpractice insurance
College tuition

HELPING THE CLIENT FIND CASH

Let's say a customer owes you a large sum of money and tells you that collections are too slow to pay you. This customer needs your help. Bruce D. Schulman is president of Niederhoffer, Cross & Zeckhauser, the nation's leading merger and acquisition firm for medium-sized companies. Schulman tells the story of escorting a Salt Lake City client to the bank and having him put up his sod farm as collateral to pay an overdue fee. Schulman took the client to dinner and heard every reason under the sun why the client could not pay, but he also heard about the sod farm—a solid asset, free of liens. The client was persuaded to meet Schulman at the bank the next morning, and within thirty minutes, the fee was being wired back to the office.

In hard times, it is likely that some of your customers or clients may be unable to pay you. They may be having cash flow problems for the same reasons you are. In this event, it is important that you do one of two things. First, you can advise them how to collect payment, to the extent of interceding on their behalf with some of their slow payers. Second, you may want to obtain a secured promissory note from a customer and discount it at your bank, thereby obtaining payment. The secured strategy will result in your getting paid only if your client is credit worthy or if the collateral that he gives you is bankable. To determine this, you may have to see the client's recent financial statements or attempt to discount the promissory note at his bank.

The first strategy is worth exploring with clients because they may not be convincing bill collectors. Ask a client what steps he has taken to persuade his customers or clients to pay. Perhaps his requests have lacked urgency. Ask him to invite his receivables clerk to join the two of you to explore various means of getting paid. If the receivables clerk has a laissez-faire attitude, you might ask permission to make a few telephone calls and to act as if you are the company's receivables clerk. If permitted by the client to speak to his slow-paying customers, you should speak very directly and to the point. As the shoemaker told Tevye in *Fiddler on the Roof*, "Just because business is slow for you, why should I suffer?" Tell the client's customer that his failure to pay has caused serious financial problems for you and that you must take whatever actions are necessary to get paid. That is the most direct way. It does not "lay a guilt trip" on the slow payer; it merely states a fact. Then ask, "How can you help me get paid?" Based on what your client's slow payer says, you can take appropriate action—with your client's permission, you can have him wire funds, agree to an assignment of his obligation via letter of credit so that you can discount it at his bank, or take legal steps if the slow payer is recalcitrant. If your client's slow payer agrees to wire transfer to your client's bank, then your client's bank can be asked to wire transfer to your bank. This will result in each party keeping accurate books, and both you and your client will get paid.

If the client rejects your offer to assist, you should use the second strategy: the secured promissory note. What do you want as collateral? The most liquid asset on the client's financial statement. A treasury bill or other liquid investment is your first choice. An investment in stocks or bonds held in a safe deposit box or at a brokerage firm is your second choice. A solid account receivable is your third choice. Some fungible equipment, such as company cars, is a fourth choice. To make absolutely certain that the client is pledging this asset to you and to no one else, you must file a UCC-1 (Uniform Commercial

Code) on that collateral in the courthouse of the county in which the company resides.

A willing client will ask his attorney to draft a UCC-1 for you. An unwilling client will make the task more difficult for you, but not impossible. You can hire a lawyer while you are in town and have him file a UCC-1 on the company's furniture, office equipment, or anything else that catches your eye during your visit. This approach will damage your relationship with your client, and it may not get you paid; however, if the client is so financially weak that it may file for bankruptcy protection, you will be in a secured position. That, as we have seen, is important.

Avoid coming away empty-handed. In the worst instance—your client throws you out of his office—hire a local attorney to collect the account receivable for you. Have your office fax all related documents to a local attorney, and ask that he proceed immediately to demand payment. If you can accomplish this by midmorning, you will still have time to fly to another city, pop in on another client, and attempt to collect the cash that you need to meet the payroll and to keep your doors open.

WHILE YOU'RE WAITING

If your manner is pleasant and your advice constructive, your client will work with you and either have a check certified or effect a wire transfer. It might take the better part of an hour to complete the mechanics of this transaction; thus, while you are waiting, you may want to do some business—raise some more cash. To do this you must be carrying in your briefcase or overnight bag all the necessary tools of the cash-raising trade: new product offerings described in a new brochure, a prototype or production model of your new upgrade product (or if that is too large and awkward to carry, then a video of the product), testimonials from other clients, and gifts. Business is a gift-giving process. Your product or service is a solution or "gift" to your customer or client. If it has a perceived value, then the client or customer will pay you your cost plus a profit. But if it lacks perceived value, then it is neither an appropriate nor an effective solution to the client's problem, and the product or service will not be ordered. Presumably, as it was ordered, the product or service has perceived value. Thus it is a gift.

As you sit in the office of your slow-paying or nonpaying client or customer, bear in mind that you are a gift-giver. To remind him of that, present him with another gift while you are in his office. If your company has a product upgrade to offer, that is the best gift you can bring. If you have a new service, that is another gift. Offer to rip up the invoice that you came to collect if the client will order and pay for the upgrade, a product that is 300 percent more expensive. Your deal is simple. You'll charge the amount of the old invoice plus 100 percent. If the service upgrade is a winner, you will walk out a winner. The rip-up-the-old-invoice gambit is a never-fail, win-win deal.

Each business is different, but the following are some general suggestions for raising more cash than you set out to get in the first place.

1. We would like to install a small computer in your office to enable you to order on-line and to receive twenty-four hour delivery.
2. We would like to install a facsimile transfer machine in your office to permit us to answer your service requests on the same day and to courier your replacement parts or add-ons the next day.
3. We have installed an 800 hotline number to permit twenty-four hour inquiries.
4. We have commissioned a market research firm to study the various ways in which our clients use our product (services), and we would like to sell you the results of the study.
5. We have a new warranty program that, for a small fee, guarantees the performance of our product for seventy-two months, or we replace it. The warranty program costs $250 per annum, or you can prepay the full amount today for a discount, and I will pick up an additional $1,000 from your controller.

These ideas may not work for you, but they might get your juices flowing. The point is that you do not see your client or customer in this office very frequently. This is quality time—a cash-collection moment. Do everything you can to load him up with gifts and suggest that more gifts are coming. In that way, you will have collected what you came for and created many reasons for more profitable contact in the future.

SUMMARY

Early in the relationship with your customers and clients establish that you want to be paid on time. Be clear and upfront. When the client exhibits slowness, get on the telephone and talk the money into your bank account. Suggest an overnight courier or a bank wire. Then, if your company hits the wall, begin offering discounts to accelerate collections from thirty days to ten days.

Visit your slow payers and help them find ways to pay you. Show them how to raise cash. While you are there, make another sale or pick up a larger check. Your customers like you, that is why they are your customers. Your clients like you more. They give you repeat business, and they want you to stay in business. Give them a win-win deal, something good for both of you. They will pay you more and more quickly.

Chapter Ten

Change Controllers

Now we turn to the liability side of your balance sheet. The objective is to stretch your payments, stretch out your stretches, and then stretch out your stretch-outs. In the center of a cash flow crisis, the person in direct contact with the irate creditors is the controller. Sometimes called the bookkeeper or the accounts payable clerk, this person handles between twenty and one hundred calls per day from anguished creditors who want a simple answer to a simple question: "When are you going to pay me?"

In the course of their business careers, creditors have heard every conceivable stall tactic. For them, "Your check is in the mail" is a dodge as old as Methuselah and about as believable. They understand cash, they are persistent and unpleasant, they keep accurate records of prior conversations and of promises either kept or broken, they know all the clever answers to clever remarks, and they don't believe anything a controller of a troubled company tells them. They live the axiom: "Get the cash before they crash."

Naturally, a controller of a troubled company can stand up to the army of credit managers, collection agencies, and commercial lawyers just so long before snapping. The controller did not create the cash flow bind. He or she will do everything possible to hold off the wolves but will run out of stretch-out plans, amusing stories, and most important, credibility, if the problem is not resolved in ninety days or so.

If your cash flow problem will not be resolved within ninety days, and if the creditors have received very little of the cash they have been telephoning daily to raise, it is time to change controllers. Your original controller is probably burned out anyway and may offer his or her resignation.

Put your nose in the *Wall Street Journal's National Employment Weekly* and contact the people with controller experience. It is not unusual to lose a controller to the burn-out plague. After all, taking creditor calls, subpoenas, and summonses all day is not child's play.

DRESS CODE FOR CONTROLLERS

When your controller visits a tough creditor, a banker, a creditor's lawyer, or the IRS, he should dress like a "schmuck." It is critical that he look like a flunky bookkeeper who is heavily numbers-oriented but not a subscriber to *Gentleman's Quarterly*. Polyester pants are a must. The short-sleeved shirt should be white, and the chest pocket should hold a plastic pen guard with three mechanical pencils and two ballpoint pens. Shoes should be cardboard-like, black lace-ups. And finally, a mismatched jacket should be worn—no matter the weather—to show a precautionary nature.

Angry bill collectors can be disarmed by an opponent who looks like a bumpkin and dresses like an ad for the Salvation Army. Disarmament is critical to the informal reorganization described in Chapter 12.

MY NAME IS GABBY HAYES

Besides dressing dumb for meetings with creditors, your controller should play dumb on the telephone as well. Why? Because *dumb is smart.* You should tell your controller to say, "I don't know where anything is," or, "I just got here, and I can't find anything."

The creditors will be nonplussed. "What do you mean you can't find anything. I've been billing you turkeys for three months, for Chrissake!"

The new controller should let the tirades pour in. Let the waves break over his head. Take the insults, the slams, the curses, and the blows. After all, the new controller did not create the debt. "I'm here to figure things out and to get you paid," he should say.

The creditors will very likely scream back, "How in the hell can you get me paid? You can't even find my invoice."

The new controller should respond, "Send me a new one," which will buy you another week.

As the new invoices arrive, you and your controller can talk about a plan of action. You should explain how deep the crisis is, whether it has bottomed out, whether there is a way out, and whether you can see the light. Let your controller know how much longer to play dumb or when to begin thinking about a payment plan. I will get to payment plans momentarily, but for now, assume that the new controller must buy you two more weeks.

He returns to his stack of phone messages and begins returning calls one by one.

"Hello. This is Gabby Hayes," the controller says as he telephones the creditors.

"Who?" the creditors ask.

(For those of you who have never heard of Gabby Hayes, he was Gene Autry's sidekick in 1950s westerns. He was befuddled by complex things, and his favorite expression was "Dag burn it!" His bafflement made all of us feel a little brighter, and we laughed with relief.)

"Who the heck is this?" the creditors ask again.

"Gabby Hayes, the new controller at XYZ Diversified," he says.

"Oh, for Pete's sake. I should have known." The creditors are relaxed and amused. They will accept a small crumb from the table. Here is the crumb.

"The boss is working on a plan to pay you guys. I haven't heard all the details, but I think you're going to like it."

"Is it cash? Is it a note? What is it?" they demand to know.

"Dag burn it! I don't know what it is."

"Then how do you know I'll like it?"

"Look, some guys aren't going to get as good a deal as you. The boss likes you. He needs your product (or service). All I know is that he said to mark your invoice *A,* and that means pay."

"When?"

"When, what?"

"When are you going to pay me?"

"I don't know. I haven't seen the plan. Let's talk tomorrow," the controller says. Then says, "Goodbye" and hangs up.

THREE TYPES OF CREDITORS

Now, the dumb stall will not work forever, nor will it work on all creditors. Creditors usually fall into three categories:

- The creditor's accounts receivable clerk
- A collection agency employee
- An attorney

The accounts receivable clerk is doing his job. Company policy will determine how much time he has to collect an account before it is written off. This period might be anywhere from 90 to 180 days, depending on a number of things such as when the creditor's fiscal year ends. The creditor's CPA firm could insist on writing off any debt over ninety days old. At this point, the debt is either sold or assigned to a collection agency.

Collection agencies such as Dun & Bradstreet are trained collectors. They are schooled in getting money out of people; it is their reason for being. However, they have time limits as well, and if they do not collect the amount owed their client within ninety days—the usual time allowed—the collectors will lose their commission or their profit.

Collectors do not know the account very well, nor do they know the historical relationship between the creditor and the customer. A clever controller can tie the collector in knots for awhile by referring to possible goods shipped back, credits to the account, improper invoices, and conversations between the company and the creditor. This line of conversation is different from what the collector is trained to say. He focuses on getting a check: when he can expect it, what the check number is, how it will be sent, whether it will be certified, and what the amount is—immediacy and specifics.

Often, the collector sits in a room with other collectors, all of them facing a wall with a thermometer on it. They all have goals. The idea is to raise the level of the thermometer to a certain dollar amount by a certain date. Their bonus is greater for faster collection of larger amounts. But occasionally, collectors go beyond good business practices. A collector once called a small company and asked to speak to the president.

"Who is calling?" asked the secretary.

"Jim Smith," the collector replied.

"From what company?" the secretary asked.

"Tell him it's about his children," the collector said.

The secretary had no choice but to put the president on the telephone. When he heard it was a collection agency, he nearly tore the telephone out of the wall. A follow-up letter to the Better Business Bureau ended the young man's career as a collector.

Collectors will find your home telephone number and badger you in the evenings and on weekends. Their favorite line is, "I will have to turn this over to legal," which is fine. If they do not collect the amount owed within a few weeks, they will lose the collection assignment to a lawyer.

When the unpaid invoice is given to a lawyer, it is not the end of the world. The lawyer may want to run up a time sheet on the matter before he settles it. In that case, he will probably begin with a long letter in which he paints a picture of the various horrors that are likely to befall you. "The plagues of Egypt will be brought on your doorstep," the letter might suggest. "Blood will spill," it may add. "Your children will grow up to despise you," might be the final inference.

Now, in fact, as long as the creditor's lawyer does not know the other creditors or their lawyers, he cannot put the company into Chapter VII by himself. If his first letter and first several phone calls do not evoke a proper response, the lawyer can file a civil suit (hiring local counsel if he is out of town). That is, he can sue on the amount owing plus legal fees and, if it is a promissory note, plus interest expenses.

The company must defend the lawsuit and file a response within thirty days. The civil suit must be properly served. You may recall in your company's bylaws that someone was designated as the "agent for service." If the process server delivers the suit to the wrong person at your company, it may not constitute proper service. Your lawyer can cite improper service in his defense of the suit, which will delay the litigation until the process server finds the "agent for service."

Your lawyer's defense will buy you a few months, until the creditor files a motion for summary judgment, which means the court is being asked to agree with the creditor and enforce payment. You must go to court and defend against a motion for summary judgment. Moreover, if your company received consideration and did not reciprocate with a payment, you will very likely lose.

I remind you that I am discussing back-to-the-wall street-fight tactics. You want to be very cautious every step of the way. If your company is not going to pull out of its nosedive, you may want to consider filing for Chapter XI instead of street fighting.

With time out for depositions and with legal fees mounting at your end, an out-of-court settlement may make more sense than getting hit with a summary judgment. Remember, once a summary judgment has been awarded, the sheriff or marshall can be sent to pick up enough of your assets—inventory, furniture, computers, file cabinets, and so forth—to pay the amount owing. With the sheriff in your office—or worse yet, a U.S. marshall who can cross county and even state lines—you will have only a few hours to raise the cash or lose valuable assets.

Gabby Hayes is not going to be effective against a rapidly encroaching lawyer. It is time to get rid of him, dag burn it!

YOU KILLED HIM!

The new controller has the task of telling the creditors that they killed Gabby.

"You killed him!" says the new controller to the creditors.

"What do you mean I killed him?" asks the creditor.

"He left a note and said he's going to do it."

"Do what?"

"We don't know. Do *it,* I guess."

"Well, I'm not sorry," says the creditor. "The little sonofabitch lied with every breath."

Now, you may find a creditor who is truly remorseful, but for the most part, creditors will take satisfaction in having accomplished something. And their satisfaction should carry the new controller a few weeks while she finds her sea legs and finds the invoices. These few weeks will permit you more time to develop a work-out plan.

VISITS TO CREDITORS

The large creditors must be visited by you. It is not wise to call them together, because they can gain courage from the presence of others of their own kind. If you have one or two very large creditors, it is imperative that you pay them the courtesy of visiting their offices. By doing so, you are showing your concern for the possible cash crunch that your inability to pay may be causing them. Printers, for instance, are particularly vulnerable to bad debts; it is not unusual for several troubled companies to owe a significant amount of money to the same printer and, at the same time, be unable to pay. If the printer, or any other creditor, must write off the debt, his own line of credit could be imperiled. Therefore, in the first stages of the visit, you will want to determine whether your tough time is causing the creditor to suffer a similar fate.

If so, you will want to ascertain whether you may be able to provide any assistance—sign a promissory note, secure it with certain unimportant assets, agree to a firm repayment plan, or the like. On the other hand, if your inability to pay is not making life difficult for the creditor, that knowledge will affect your repayment plan.

Ninety-five percent of the success you will achieve in your negotiations with large creditors will be determined by the amount of preparation you put into the meeting. For heaven's sake, don't wing it. It is critical that you prepare a detailed cash flow statement to show how the creditor will be paid if he goes along with your redirect-and-grow plan (see Chapter 12). It is also important that the creditor receive a recent, unaudited balance sheet and a current operating statement. These should be handed to the creditor with your explanation of why you are unable to pay him.

Point out to the creditor that there will be nothing for him if your company is forced into Chapter VII. Point out that Chapter XI is a possibility but that you strongly prefer to avoid it because of the effect it would have on sales, on collecting accounts receivable, and on your company's ability to conduct business in a usual and customary manner.

As one of your largest creditors, therefore, it is important to you and to your informal reorganization that the creditor accept your stretch-out plan. If he goes along, then you must believe you can sell it to others. If he does not go along, you will have to file for protection and convince a bankruptcy judge to cram down the plan. That will be expensive for everyone, and you would rather pay your bills than pay lawyers.

It is true that if the large creditors accept your stretch-out plan, most of the small creditors—to whom you owe less than $5,000—will probably go along with it. If not, you can handle several $5,000 creditors better than you can handle several $200,000 ones. Victory will come if you follow these suggestions:

1. Prepare extensively for the meeting.
2. Bring cash flow projections and financial statements with you.
3. Bring photographs or samples of the new product line that is going to generate the increase in sales.

4. If your bail-out plan involves the leveraged buy-out of a company with positive cash flow, bring financial statements, descriptive materials, and cash flow projections of the target company.
5. Determine whether you have hurt the creditor, and, if you have, spend time developing a strategy to protect the creditor's line of credit or financial well-being.
6. Do not be in a hurry to present your plan and leave. Stay until you receive an answer. Come back the next day if that is necessary.
7. Be sure your office does not call you at the creditor's office; rather, at an appropriate time, call your office for messages. If you receive phone calls, it could give the appearance that your ship has too many leaks.
8. Be clear, truthful, precise, and professional. Approach the negotiation of the stretch-out plan with gravity and seriousness.

The angle at which you come out of your cash crisis—standing up or laid out flat—depends a great deal on your negotiating skills with your large creditors. One of the great teachers of negotiation, Somers H. White, continually reminds his students that in a negotiation, *he who has the most time wins.* This is important because you have, in fact, very little time to spend with one of many creditors. On the other hand, if you do not give the large creditors all the time they require to come to the conclusion you want, you will very likely not have the time to complete your rescue plan—LBO, new direct-marketing scheme, seminar selling, new product introduction, or whatever. Therefore, you must camp on the creditor's doorstep until you have convinced him of the following:

- You cannot pay him immediately
- You cannot pay him in six to twelve months
- In Chapter VII, he will lose everything
- In Chapter XI, after years of discussion and debate, your plan will be crammed down anyway at great legal expense to everyone
- If he goes along with your stretch-out plan, you are certain that you can convince others to do so as well

A final note of caution: do not reveal the names of creditors to other creditors. They may gang up on you and force you into Chapter VII.

THE PREGNANCY

I was advising a company in a work-out situation a few years ago, and I got into the picture a little late. The creditors were enraged, and many of the obligations had been turned over to lawyers. We needed all the creditors to back off for two months, permitting management to develop and implement an informal plan of reorganization. How do you buy two months?

We installed a new controller, and she was in her seventh month of pregnancy. She introduced herself on the telephone and very appropriately said that the invoices would have to be pulled together so that within a week or so, she would know the accounts pretty well. There were four hundred individual obligations, and she was unfamiliar with them, but it would not take her too long.

"By the way," she added, "I'm going to have a baby fairly soon."

There is no credit manager, collection agent, or commercial lawyer on the face of the earth who does not love babies or revere the miracle of giving birth. The thought that they might adversely affect the successful delivery of a baby changed their entire approach to the matter of collecting the money owed them.

"A baby? And you're doing this job?" they asked.

"Yes, my first."

"When is it due?"

"In two months."

The die was cast. The creditors realized they were not going to hassle this sweet young lady who would have her first child in sixty days. Many stopped calling. A handful hung in there and scratched away for nickels and dimes; but, for the most part, the company bought the two months it needed.

When the controller left two weeks before the baby was due, another voice handled the calls. More questions were asked about Donna's condition than about possible payment and payment dates. By the time the baby was born, the company was well on its way with a stretch-out plan.

ETHICS

Do you invent a pregnant controller if you do not have one? Do you invent a recovery plan if you do not have one? What are the ethics of dealing with creditors?

The Golden Rule and the Ten Commandments provide the ethical baseline. If you are trying to convert suppliers and lenders to long-term partners, convince them to own your stock, or convince them to take ten-year notes, there is no way to succeed unless your ethics are of the very highest order. A lie, a misrepresentation, a flim-flam, or any other form of trickery will be transparent to your creditors. The only solution is to be perfectly honest. Never promise anything you cannot deliver. Stick to the truth; it is easier to remember.

On the other hand, just as you would not tell the referee in a hard-fought basketball game that you walked or that you fouled a player on the other team, so you would not reveal every nuance of your crisis to your creditors. They do not need to know, and if they did know, you could foul out of the game. As in any sport, you are playing to win, and you can play as hard as you like as long as you play fair.

SUMMARY

Change controllers in order to buy time. You have put several cash-generating plans into play, but they need time to light up the scoreboard. You have designed a stretch-out plan, but you need time to sell it to creditors and their lawyers. Thus, you need time. New voices gain time. New controller stories gain time.

Even so, some creditors will need personal visits. It is your choice whether to send your controller or to go yourself. If your controller makes the visit, make certain that he dresses and acts like Harvey Milktoast, the timid bean counter. You should visit the large, significant creditors—the ones that are bigger than you. They can outspend you in court, and they can force you to divert cash from product to lawyers. Before visiting them, prepare thoroughly for the meeting, and understand their needs. Unveil your redirect-and-grow plan to them. Make them a partner in your work-out plan if you can.

Chapter Eleven

Play the Float

Hard-pressed small companies learn to stretch their dollars by paying toward the end of the week, mailing from remote places, and asking the bank to telephone the company before bouncing a check. In tough times, you will need to maintain at least three bank accounts. One is the major account, used to pay suppliers, and it is floated continually. The checkbook always shows an overdraft, whereas the balances at the bank are generally positive. When they are negative, the bank calls to say, "Wire money in or we have to send back some checks." This account is stretched to the limit and then some. Wire into it from your safe bank as needed.

The second account is never overdrawn. It is used to pay certain bills promptly, to pay certain payroll items, and to pay critical accounts that cannot be late and that cannot bounce. The second account has a small but stable balance in it, and it is replenished as needed. It is maintained at a second bank, and if there exists a threat of prejudgment attachment, this second bank is an independent bank in the next county.

The third account is your safety-valve account; it is out of state and preferably in a town to which you travel. It has a small, inviolate balance in it for last-ditch emergencies.

THE PERMITTED OVERDRAFT

In the early stages of their company's growth, company managers should meet with their bankers to win favor and support. The manager may need the bank to allow the company to be overdrawn occasionally and, just as important, to allow the company to write checks on uncollected funds. If you treat the banker fairly and do not misuse the privileges or accommodations granted, the bank may be willing to be even more generous in the future and may even loan you some serious money.

The bank that loans you money does not want to see you file for protection; it will stretch. Keep the loan officer up-to-date on your plans. Remember to mail him your publicity concerning grants or new product introductions. Make him part of your plan. Pay the loan down every opportunity you get.

Consequently, unless the commercial bank is stodgy and conservative—in which case you should not be giving them your deposits—you will have a sympathetic ear at your commercial bank. You want to build a relationship so that the banker knows your company's goals and objectives and knows your progress toward meeting them. This relationship is built with information and solidified with acts of friendship.

An officer at the lowest rung of a commercial bank begins with modest authority, perhaps the ability to loan $25,000 without prior approval, the right to permit overdrafts, and the ability to give instant credit on deposits that might otherwise require seven to ten days to clear. You should never bounce a check, of course, but if a deposit is bounced to you or is delayed by weather or by unforeseen circumstances, and if you had to pay the company's health insurance or the utility bill rather than risk a cut-off, then it is appropriate to ask your banker to pay rather than bounce your check. If you have established good lines of communication with your banker, he or she will protect your account.

IMMEDIATE CREDIT FOR DEPOSITS

The same can be said about obtaining immediate credit on noncash deposits. If the banker has been kept well informed by you and knows your financial statements fairly well, then he or she will probably treat checks written to your company as cash deposits. The exceptions would be if your deposits were drawn on foreign banks or if a meaningful number of them bounced from time to time.

Obtaining immediate credit is the equivalent of having a line of credit to draw down on for seven to ten days while the checks clear. When a banker provides this service to your company, he or she is foregoing earning interest on that line of credit. Thus, at some point in time, you will have to reciprocate the bank's generosity.

WHAT BILLS TO PAY AND WHEN

In order to save as much of your capital as possible, you and your controller should spend a few hours together reviewing the accounts payable in order to stretch them as far as possible. The utility companies—telephone, electric, gas, or oil—hook you up without a credit reference, but if payment arrives at their office one day after the cut-off notice, they will disconnect you. Then, if you want to have the service restored, it may be necessary to put up a deposit. Stretching these particular accounts payable beyond their absolute cut-off days will cost you capital, and you will lose two or more positive credit references.

Health insurance is a service that employees frequently regard with the kind of veneration they attach to a regular paycheck. You cannot sacrifice health insurance. However, you can cancel life insurance and disability policies. Be clear with all your employees when you do this. Tell them the choice is payroll or insurance. They will prefer payroll.

With the rising costs of health insurance, some companies are looking for less expensive ways to insure. Contact the local HMOs to see whether they can improve on your health insurance costs. You might ask a person who is knowledgeable about indemnity carriers and HMOs to help you with this analysis.

Courier services are difficult to live without, as are your photostat and postage machines. Facsimile transfer machines are becoming a part of the business scene as well. When is the last time you reviewed the service or rental contracts on these critical services and indispensable pieces of office equipment? How late can you pay for these services without losing them? Sixty days? Ninety days? In the event your company falls through the floor during the recession, it would be smart to know how far you can stretch these payment obligations. You may be able to switch from one vendor to another and gain ninety days of free service.

Invoices from suppliers are generally bills representing products shipped or services provided to your company in good faith—in the belief that you would pay within the time agreed. Unlike the electric bill or the telephone bill, your suppliers will not cut you off for failure to pay in thirty days; they will work with you, to a point. Until you get deeply in trouble, you will not know what that point is. However, rest assured that slow payment of your accounts payable is one of the cheapest forms of capital—the other is customer financing (see Chapter 3).

But how slow can you be? Perhaps there is an industry standard, and you are paying your bills twice as fast as your competitors. If you are doing this, then you are providing inexpensive capital to your suppliers.

HOW FAR TO STRETCH

If your suppliers are publicly held, it would prove instructive to order their annual reports to see how rapidly their accounts receivable turn over. Assume the annual report of a major supplier of component parts resembles Table 11.1.

Table 11.1   *Annual Report of a Major Supplier*

Item	12/31/86 ($000)	12/31/87 ($000)
Revenues, net	$150,000	$200,000
Accounts receivable	$20,000	$30,000
Accounts receivable turnover	7.5×	6.7×
Accounts receivable days on hand	48.7 days	54.5 days

You will notice that your important supplier has driven its sales up in the prior year by over 30 percent, perhaps at the expense of extending more favorable terms to its customers. Average accounts receivable days on hand increased from forty-nine to fifty-five days, an increase of a little more than 10 percent. With this knowledge of your supplier, it might be possible for you to let your payments slide a week without incurring the supplier's wrath.

If your supplier is a privately held company, you may have difficulty determining its sales and accounts receivable. The following are some investigative tips to help you construct financial information about a privately held company.

1. *Dun & Bradstreet.* You can subscribe to this service, but it is relatively expensive, and the information is not all that reliable. Do you remember what you told Dun & Bradstreet about your company? Chances are your report was neither thorough nor accurate, and it probably overstated net worth. Ask a friend at a bank to order a Dun & Bradstreet report for you, and save the $800 sign-up fee plus the $28.50 charge per report.

2. *Local Newspaper Articles.* Most companies with sales of $5 million or more have been written about in their hometown newspapers. Telephone the newspapers in your creditor's city and ask if an article has been written about them. If so, order it.

3. *Parking Lot Test.* Ask a friend in the creditor's city to drive by the plant and to give you a parking lot count. Assume 1.5 employees per car and multiply the employees by $100,000 in order to get an approximation of your creditor's sales.

4. *Just Ask.* This is one of my favorite expressions. People frequently fail to ask the question that is uppermost in their minds. But not you. You need to know, so just ask. "Are we your slowest payable? Do most companies pay you in forty-five days? What percentage go beyond forty-five days?" You will be surprised what accounts receivable clerks will tell you if you just ask.

5. *Checking Bank References.* Your bank can verify the credit worthiness of the supplier for you. Bankers have a

code of ethics stating that one bank will not withhold credit information from another bank if the request is reasonably made. For instance, the purpose for which the request is made must be legitimate and not merely curiosity. In your case, ask your banker to check the financial strength of Precision Components Corporation because you will be relying on it to ship you an important component part each month.

6. *High Five.* By using Polk's and Dun & Bradstreet's codes, your banker will quickly reach your supplier's bank and get a verbal report: "Precision Components maintains balances with us that average high five figures. It has had a borrowing relationship with us since mid-1985 of moderate to medium seven figures. The relationship is very satisfactory." That is a very positive reference. What the supplier's bank said was that the company's checking account averages $80,000 to $99,000, that the company borrows from $1.2 million to $1.6 million, and that it pays the bank a regular and profitable interest rate.

SUMMARY

The stronger your suppliers' financial health, the more you can lean on them. The faster they are spinning their capital, the less you can stretch them. Continually gather information on your suppliers. Clip articles from the trade journals and maintain a scrap book.

Remember that if you have to visit them to negotiate a stretch-out, your knowledge about them will be very impressive and will heighten your credibility with them. By switching suppliers of office equipment and by changing couriers, you may be able to pick up ninety days of credit on these accounts. There are other creditors that you can pay slowly if you know their industries' payment terms.

Never make "your check is in the mail" promises unless they are true. Your credibility with creditors will be tested when you sell your informal reorganization plan. Unkept promises made today will hurt you tomorrow.

CREATING AND EXECUTING A REDIRECT-AND-GROW PLAN

Chapter Twelve

The Survival Strategies

We now enter the synthesis or rebuilding stage. The company has hit the bottom of the roller coaster. The enemies are known, the bullets that can put the company in the boneyard have been identified, cash has been raised and husbanded, teammates have been chosen, time has been bought and used, and back-to-the-wall street-fight tactics have been resorted to when needed. The company is ready to spring back like a shot and soar to new heights of achievement and profitability. So here is the rebuilding plan.

The president and the chief financial officer should meet on a Sunday and thoroughly analyze the company's cash position. The amount of available or raisable cash and an assessment of the bullets that could strike the company (which determines the size of the needed reserve) will determine which strategies can be selected for the redirect-and-grow plan. If there is only enough cash on hand for ninety days—twelve to fourteen weeks—a grant proposal may not be practical. Perhaps the technology should be licensed or sold outright. The proceeds could be plowed into finding and buying an LBO target. If there is only enough cash on hand for sixty days, a bankruptcy lawyer should probably be retained so that, if needed, the company can be put quickly into Chapter XI. An LBO can be achieved out of Chapter XI, and don't forget the option to go public via the Chapter XI route. In any event all strategies emanate from the cash flow statement.

CASH FLOW STATEMENTS AS ROAD MAPS

In every battle plan there is a map of the area. The map points out the enemy position and topographical elements. Similarly, the cash flow statement points out the most serious bills, the next most serious, and all the others. It also indicates your sources of cash to meet these obligations. It is your battle plan, and you must update it weekly throughout the crisis period.

You will be carrying out a strategy to preserve the company and to thrust it forward as an exciting new business. You have begun a new chase. It is the survive and thrive game, and you are the team leader. I call the chase the *redirect-and-grow* plan. Simultaneously, you and your controller will be negotiating a stretch-out plan for the liabilities that the company will pay with the cash flow generated by the accomplishments of the redirect-and-grow plan. Let's refer to this stretch-out process as the *informal reorganization* plan.

Two plans will be operating in tandem. Tactically, you must appoint one leader for each plan. Perhaps the president could lead the redirect-and-grow plan while his or her second-in-command can head up the informal reorganization plan. The weekly cash flow statement will be the playing field; the ball, bat, and gloves will be the tools that you have learned in this book; and the character of the players will include the heart, courage, judgment, and business acumen that you and your teammates have developed in your business careers. Those careers were spring training compared with the contest you are about to compete in.

WHY TEAMS

Survival is a game. It has winners and losers. The winners are those companies that become *ready*—that establish their objectives clearly and carry them out in as near to militaristic precision as possible. The informal reorganization team will need at least three members to make calls on the creditors, and two assistants to prepare the promissory notes, cover letters, and other communications. If the number of creditors exceeds five hundred, the informal reorganization team will need another member to sell the plan and another assistant for communications.

The redirect-and-grow team will need at least two members and one assistant for every two cash-generating plans that it implements. Let's assume you decide that the redirect-and-grow plan will be twofold, including (1) an LBO and (2) an RDLP (Research and Development Limited Partnership) for a new product. The LBO is expected to generate sufficient cash to meet all of the creditor obligations over several years; the RDLP is intended to raise enough capital to finance the development of a dramatic innovation that will offer an inexpensive solution to a large problem shared by many. It would be an unexpected plus if the innovative product could be marketed by the LBO target, but perfection is not your goal; mere success will suffice.

You can see immediately that devoting full time and quality time to both redirect-and-grow plans is required because of their complexity; their networking requirements; the involvement of accountants, lawyers, and investment bankers; and the need for accuracy. A three-person team plus a word-processing assistant are the minimum number required to consummate the redirect-and-grow plans. If a third plan is added—such as spinning off a division, selling a foreign license, or beginning a direct-mail marketing activity—additional team members will have to be added. However, too many redirect-and-grow plans will diffuse the company's efforts, and nothing will get accomplished. In that event, the informal reorganization plan, which must be so carefully sold to creditors, will have to be resold on less attractive terms. This is called stretching the stretch-out. It can be done if the redirect-and-grow plan is in high gear; otherwise, it is a tough sell.

TEAM MEMBERS

For the redirect-and grow team—assuming the two plans are to "buy something" and to "start a development project"—it would seem prudent that the team members include the president, the house counsel, and the chief scientific officer. If the plans are to "sell something" and to "open new marketing channels," the chief scientific officer should be replaced with the chief marketing officer. The team members should occupy a conference room at the company—and possibly a conference room in your lawyer's office when the deals appear to be near closing. All documents necessary to carry out the plans should be maintained in an orderly manner in the conference room, with back-up copies at the company's law firm and with the word-processing operator.

The informal reorganization team should be headed by the number two person in the company or the chief financial officer, and it should include the number two financial person and the chief marketing officer (or if he is already on the redirect-and-grow team, the number two marketing person). This team should use a room in which they can see one another and communicate with one another about the acceptance of the stretch-out plan by creditors. A conference room is not ideal because it might get noisy and unwieldy. A large room with five or six desks and telephones is perhaps the best arrangement.

CHARTING THE TWO STRATEGIES

The events and cash flows of the redirect-and-grow strategy will impact the informal reorganization strategy; therefore it is necessary to chart the two strategies rather than operate them independently. Let's make certain assumptions about the nature of the company's crisis and the strategies it selects for bailing itself out.

1. *Nature of the Crisis.* Let's assume the company had sales of $15 million and small earnings in the previous year. Management expected sales to increase by 20 percent, so it plowed everything back into advertising and marketing, including a $1 million secured loan. But instead of sales increasing, they slid off and are now running at an annual rate of $7.5 million. A recession pulled the wheels off of the company's wagon. Company management responded slowly to the crisis, first denying it, then becoming angry, and finally resolving to try to save the company. (Sharp downturns are rarely recognized as precursors of doom when they first occur.) Finally, the realization that the company was out of business began to set in, but too late. Virtually every receivable had been collected, and the company was out of inventory. Layoffs were effected after the fact. So now the cupboard is just about bare.

   The company owes $3.8 million to four hundred creditors, including the $1 million secured loan to a bank. The company's customers have gone elsewhere. A product upgrade would be well received, but more design and development are needed; then, a strong dose of telemarketing and direct-mail would be needed to generate large orders.

2. *The Appropriateness of the Informal Reorganization.* The company's remaining inventory can be sold to a jobber for $400,000. The remaining accounts receivable are owed by deadbeats and can be turned over to a collection agent. Some equipment, vans, and furniture can be sold for about $150,000. Thus, in liquidation, the company would show assets of $550,000 and liabilities of $3.8 million. The bank would receive 55 percent of the loan, or $550,000, less legal fees in a Chapter VII, and all the other creditors would be left empty-handed. A Chapter XI plan or reorganization would chew up perhaps one-third of the $550,000 war chest in legal fees. Therefore, the appropriate strategy is the informal reorganization. It husbands the $550,000, which permits the company a certain amount of time to consummate its turnaround plan. Just how much time is available depends on some worst-case cash flow projections, but anything over 120 days is enough to uncork a redirect-and-grow plan.

3. *Dual Redirect-and-Grow Plan—Buy Something and Develop Something.* The company's senior management reviews the myriad of options that were discussed previously—buy, sell, add channels, fill existing channels, develop something, leverage something, leverage the customers, and so on. Management adopts a dual redirect-and-grow strategy with the notion that if one fails, the other will back it up. The first strategy is to buy a company with positive cash flow, using LBO financing techniques. The cash flow from the LBO target can be applied to the $3.8 million of indebtedness, and the remaining cash flow can be applied to direct-mail or telemarketing. The team approves the dual plan, and everyone is excited by it. After ninety days of trench fighting, it is time to rebuild a new company. Victory is in sight. The "buy something" strategy is selected because the recession has produced many sellers at relatively inexpensive prices. The second strategy, to develop an upgrade product using funds provided by a state grant, is selected because the company has visited the state's economic development director and determined that it meets the criteria for about $1 million in funding.

4. *Manpower.* Your war buddies are seven hale and hearty souls who will walk bare-footed through hell for the company. They are arranged as in Table 12.1.

Clearly, you can assign more people to the teams, and this is highly recommended for larger companies. But it is my experience that two small teams made up of players with the characteristics described in Chapter 2—players who will fight

Table 12.1   Team Arrangement

Redirect-and-Grow	Product Upgrades	Informal Reorganization
President	Chief scientific officer	VP marketing
Chief financial officer		Second financial officer
Secretary-word processor		Secretary-word processor

day and night for the company—form the optimal configuration.

In the course of a six-month turnaround plan, the seven people will necessarily work at reduced salaries, until the first breakthrough occurs in the plan. Remember, the $550,000 must cover payroll, overhead, travel, communications costs, and legal fees for 120 to 150 days. Several other employees are necessarily kept on board for creditor calls, collections, and various odd jobs, all at reduced salaries until the light appears at the end of the tunnel. It is a tight budget; it will require excellent internal communications as well as cooperation in order to win the survival game with so small a war chest.

To gain an advantage, the seven-person team will have to put in more time. The players will have to agree to work on Sunday afternoons to compare their performance to the time charts and to create a new cash flow statement each week.

The time chart is a large calendar that has performance dates flagged at certain times in the future. For example, a letter of intent with a seller should be signed in thirty days, financing for the LBO should be raised in sixty days, the grant application should be filed in fourteen days, and funding of the grant should be received in ninety days. The team leaders are responsible for meeting these deadlines. If the team suffers a slip-up, the leader should put the team on overtime until it catches up. Time is as important as cash at this stage.

The LBO strategy gets underway immediately with the search for and analysis of target sellers. In the first thirty days of the turnaround, the informal reorganization team does not unveil its stretch-out plan to creditors, because it is awaiting greater definition from the redirect-and-grow team. (Remember to introduce a new voice to talk to the creditors at this time in order to buy another thirty days.) Although creditors have not received a dime in ninety days, the informal reorganization team will have to "tap dance" for another thirty days. No more "Gabby Hayes," no more pregnant controllers. The object now is to create a curiosity and an excitement about the stretch-out plan before unveiling it—like showing coming attractions before the feature movie.

PREPARE YOUR CASH FLOW
STATEMENTS ON SUNDAYS

The team members must continually gauge themselves against the available funds in the war chest. Each Sunday a new cash flow statement should be prepared with extreme attention to detail—rivaling that of a brain surgeon. The object of the continual updating of weekly cash flow statements is to keep generating cash to meet emergencies.

For example, assume that you begin with $550,000 in cash (in your out-of-country banks, partially on deposit, and partially in a money-market account). In your first cash flow projection, you allocated the money as in Table 12.2.

Murphy's Law augurs poorly for a company in crisis, and you can bet that the $174,000 will be chipped away by eager-beaver lawyers representing creditors who heard the "Gabby Hayes" routine one time too many. A writ of attachment occurs on the day you wire in payroll, and the sheriff plucks $50,000 from under your mattress. But you and your team are alive and energized. You'll find another $50,000 somewhere. Then the LBO aborts, and $75,000 is gone—spent for legal, accounting,

Table 12.2 First Cash Flow Projection

Accounts Payable	Amount
Seven team members for five months	$120,000
Six support personnel for five months	60,000
FICA, insurance	36,000
Utilities	10,000
Telephone	10,000
Rent	30,000
Postage, couriers	5,000
Travel	10,000
Legal fees	15,000
LBO upfront fees, expenses	75,000
Consumables, supplies	5,000
Subtotal	376,000
Reserve to meet emergencies	174,000
Total	$550,000

appraisal, and bank commitment fees. You have to go find another LBO target and another $70,000. You'll do it.

Assume then that you have used up $125,000 of the $174,000 reserve and that the redirect-and-grow team is ninety days away from completing a new LBO, which will generate positive cash flow. Worse still your banker telephones to say that his auditors have insisted you pay three months' back interest—$30,000—immediately, or he will have to begin fore-closure proceedings. You have the cash. It's in payroll reserve. But if you invade that war chest, you're just shooting yourself in the foot.

Here is what you do. Bring your six war buddies into the conference room, and brainstorm: where can you find $30,000 for the banker by tomorrow, plus another $125,000 to replenish the emergency reserve?

Review the earlier chapters on schlepping, sale leasebacks, and other cash-raising tactics. The ideas will leap out at you. Sell the word-processing computers to a leasing company and rent them back for a $30,000 windfall. Sell your frequent flyer points to ticket brokers—each 60,000 points generates about $600 in cash. Lay off two support people, and ask the others to double up. Sell shelving for scrap value. Rent office and ware-house space to other companies. Take out second mortgages on your homes in exchange for warrants or future cash bonuses. Pawn jewelry. Cancel insurance policies. Ask relatives for ninety-day loans. Ask your lawyer to work for stock; this could save $20,000. Then modify the cash flow statement projections, and assign forty-eight-hour emergency-cash-raising duties to each of the team members. Buy a bottle of champagne, and throw a small party when the $125,000 is found three days later. You will all deserve it!

THE STRETCH-OUT PLAN

When either the "buy something" or the "develop something" plan appears to be working, it is time to announce to the creditors how you plan to pay them and when. As a first step, the four hundred creditors should be organized according to the following categories of criticality:

A—Priority claims, taxes
B—Secured creditors
C—Unsecured creditors, over $25,000
D—Unsecured creditors, $10,000 to $24,999
E—Unsecured creditors, $1,000 to $9,999
F—Unsecured creditors, under $999
G—Special exceptions

You may have another arrangement in mind, particularly if there is a bulge in the $1,000-to-$9,999 group, and it must be broken up into two categories. The object of grouping the creditors into categories is to offer them differing repayment plans.

Assume that the LBO target will be able to provide a postacquisition cash flow of $200,000 per month to the company. To be conservative, plan on having only half, or $100,000 per month. Then use half of that number, $50,000, to pay the salaries and benefits of the survival team and another $25,000 for utilities, legal fees, and general and administrative expenses. If the "develop something" strategy has been successful, then the survival team has an additional 3 to 5 percent (of the grant) available in the form of a project management fee. Save this money, because it will serve as telemarketing and direct-mail marketing dollars when the product upgrade is ready.

The cash available to pay the $3.8 million in debt is one-half of the LBO's cash flow, or $100,000 per month. If all creditors are paid equally, it will take thirty-eight months to repay $3.8 million (say forty-eight months, to leave yourself a cushion and to pay interest). However, the smaller creditors may not go along with a forty-eight-month plan because the individual payments to them will be very small, and their need for cash is usually very great. You may have to offer them cents on the dollar or a twelve-month stretch. Creditors owed $5,000 to $10,000 are usually difficult to deal with. They will need some careful negotiating. The larger creditors can take a longer stretch plus an interest rate and perhaps an upside opportunity such as warrants in consideration for their forebearance. Therefore, an effective stretch-out plan recognizes the needs of all the creditors as well as the degree to which they can be leveraged.

Common Stock

Do not rule out the possibility of offering common stock to your creditors for all or part of the amount owing. If your survival team has been clear, intelligent, open, and forthright, if the LBO target has an interesting story—hopefully a solid, dependable cash flow without a requirement for capital expenditures—and if the product upgrade story has an excitement, there is absolutely no reason not to try selling your stock to your creditors. Tell them that fortunes are made in adversity. The creditors who will be needed to sell you the components for your product upgrade are the most likely to accept common stock rather than a promissory note paid out over forty-eight months.

Promissory Note

Another plan might include five series of promissory notes— with or without options to convert them into common stock— with interest at a very low rate—5 to 7 percent—payable in the forty-eighth month. The larger the creditor, the longer the term. However, there may be special exceptions such as the creditor whom you need badly as a supplier, but who will go out of business unless he is paid more quickly. This creditor is in category G. The upside, or sweetener, might be to accelerate the note if the company's earnings increase dramatically. An alternative upside might be to have the balance of the note convertible into common stock; then, if earnings drop dramatically, the loyal creditors who convert a large portion of their note into stock could make a pile of money on your adversity.

Communicating the Stretch-Out Plan

We have discussed the need to visit your bank and the large, important creditors. We have also discussed the most effective means of presenting the stretch-out plan via telephone. What follows then is the promissory note that you would like them to sign and return to you, plus the cover letter that accompanies it. A sample cover letter and promissory note have been tailored to the example we have been studying, and they appear in Appendices I and II.

SUMMARY

There is something special about the thrill of balancing a dangerous situation in terrible times. There is an exhilaration in effecting an informal reorganization and a redirect-and-grow plan successfully. It is chaotic, cacophonous, and fraught with danger. The smallest win—getting your first signed note back in the mail—is like a snowfall on Christmas Day. There is a certain beauty in adroitly dodging the threats from lawyers. There is pure delight in winning white-knuckled negotiations with LBO sellers. Nothing in business equals the joy of a forty-eight-hour cash-finding crisis that ends with cash in the bank. These times cannot be matched by any other business experience. You'll remember them as your finest hour.

Conclusion

You have not gained battle scars from reading this book, but you have achieved the next best thing. You are ready. You are psychologically prepared. You are a pioneer mother about to rebuild the farm and end up owning fifty head of cattle.

Your company may experience sudden devastation due to product obsolescence. Your region may be ruined when a major employer fails. A severe industry turndown could surprise you, or a nationwide recession could force your back to the wall. But you will be ready. Damn right!

You understand crisis-intervention. You know the difference between a stressor—a crisis-provoking event—and a genuine crisis. You understand how to select those war buddies who have the heart to stick with you and how to get rid of those who should be terminated. You have fully informed your lieutenants. You have studied your creditors' strengths and needs. You know which bullets might come and when they might strike.

We have dealt in some detail with the components of a survive-and-thrive plan. You have learned the "buy something" strategy, and you know how to use LBO techniques to buy a weak competitor or a frightened company. You have learned how to fund a development project with state, RDLP, or grant money. You have learned how to buy time and how to leverage customers, suppliers, and lenders. If you are forced into bankruptcy, you have learned how to use that as a means of going public and as a way of implementing our redirect-and-grow plan.

Even if your friendly, helpful banker leaves, and the new banker tries to clean up all the old loans by obtaining a writ of attachment, you are ready with multiple bank accounts in diverse locations. Even if your new controller buys you time to set your redirect-and-grow plans in motion, but there are delays, and you need more time, you are ready to change controllers again. You know how to gauge the needs of your most critical creditors, the ones who must go along with your stretch-out plan in order for it to succeed. You know how to learn as much as possible about them before visiting them in person. You have learned how to outline your informal reorganization and redirect-and-grow plans. You know how to set up your two teams, chart your strategies, and create your weekly cash flow statements.

The war chest is in a protected money market account, and it is the dawn of the day of your launch. You have "made much of the negatives." You are ready to springboard to a new and higher level of financial success. Your team is excited by the prospect of putting the redirect-and-grow plan into effect. Your company went down the roller coaster of crisis at a dizzying speed, but your survival team is accelerating to a level of reorganization and success higher than you ever dreamed was possible.

So let the bottom drop.

You're ready!

Cover Letter Seeking Creditor Agreement to an Informal Reorganization

Date: _____

_____
_____
_____
_____

Dear: _____

Following our recent telephone conversation, Survival Management Corporation (SMC) and its subsidiary, Survival Product Upgrade Corporation, have been unable to meet their obligations. Further, the situation has deteriorated; SMC owes in excess of $3.8 million and has assets of less than $300,000, all of which are claimed by a secured creditor. The situation does not lend itself to a Chapter XI reorganization or to a Chaper VII wind-up and liquidation because there would be virtually no pay-out to unsecured creditors.

215

Page 2

As a result, SMC intends to effect an informal reorganization, repaying its creditors over time. The company has two assets that make an informal reorganization and a repayment program possible: a seasoned management team that refuses to give up, and a customer base of over 20,000 users who we believe will purchase our product upgrades.

SMC has located a company in a related business and intends to purchase that company via a leveraged buy-out, using debt secured by the new company's assets and a note convertible into SMC stock. After allowing for repayment on the leveraged buy-out financing, the new combined company will generate a positive cash flow. It is from this cash flow that SMC will repay you and its other creditors.

However, as a condition of the merger, we must receive approval from *all* of SMC's creditors for a restructuring of SMC's debt. We propose, therefore, to convert the indebtedness to a four-year note bearing interest at 7.5 percent per annum as set forth in the attached promissory note.* The attached promissory note includes a limited release (Note and Release) from you to enable the acquisition.

In this informal reorganization, it is essential that we receive your approval for the plan. If we cannot effect the merger, we will be forced to liquidate SMC for the benefit of the secured creditor, leaving you and other creditors with almost nothing.

Please consider our offer as a sincere attempt to repay you in full with interest, and please vote in favor of this plan. To agree to the terms outlined in the Note and Release, please sign the attached blank Note and Release where indicated, and return it to us by August 14, 19____. We will then send you the executed Note and Release. (The extra copy is for your records until the fully executed Note and Release is returned to you.)

Send Note and Release to my attention at

> Your Name
> Survival Management Corporation
> Your Address
> City, State, Zip Code

---

* This language varies at this point for each category of creditor.

Page 3

If we have creditor consent to this plan, payments will begin October 31, 19_____. Without consent, we will be forced to file for protection under Chapter VII of the Bankruptcy Act and liquidate the Company, in which event you will not receive payment on the indebtedness.*

Sincerely yours,

Your Name
Chairman

Enclosure: Note and Release (2)

---

* Accompanying this letter is the Promissory Note and Release (see Appendix II). The value of the "buy something" and "develop something" strategies is that extra little suggestion of leverage: the seller of the LBO target wants 100 percent of the creditors to approve the stretch-out plan, or the state wants 100 percent acceptance of the plan before it funds. Do not forget to add this little incentive, as I have done in paragraph 4.

Nonnegotiable Promissory Note and Release

Holder: _____

Address: _____

_____

Principal Amount: $_____ Due: _____

FOR VALUE RECEIVED, Survival Management Corporation, a Delaware corporation (hereinafter "the Company" or "SMC"), its successors, and assigns, whose address is *Your Address, City, State, Zip Code*, hereby promise to pay, subject to the conditions set forth below, to Holder* above at the address set forth above, or such other place(s) as the Holder shall direct, the principal sum set forth above plus interest of seven and one-half percent (7.5%) per annum for four (4) years payable as follows: forty-eight (48) equal monthly install-ments of $_____each, the first installment to be paid December 31, 19____, subsequent installments to be paid monthly thereafter;

plus

if the Company's pretax annual earnings for any of the next ten years exceed $5.0 million, a payment of $_____, representing the

---

* The word *Payee* may be used in place of *Holder*.

Page 2

balance of the principal and interest due and unpaid for the period of four (4) years beginning December 31, 19____, to be paid ninety (90) days after the thirty-sixth (36th) monthly payment is made hereunder.

In the event of default by the Company in performance of this Note and Release or in payment of any amount or installment of principal and interest to the Holder of this Note, the Holder of this Note shall be entitled to acceleration of the balance of principal and interest of this Note. Upon declaration of acceleration by the Holder hereof, the entire balance of principal and interest shall become due and payable in full, subject to the conditions set forth below. Other rights, powers, privileges, and remedies of the Holder of this Note are cumulative and not exclusive of any rights, powers, remedies, and privileges that the Holder might have.

Notwithstanding anything herein to the contrary, the Company covenants and agrees with the Holder, and the Holder covenants by acceptance hereof, expressly for the benefit of the present and future holders of "Senior Indebtedness," defined as any debt due and owing in connection with the acquisition of entities to be acquired by SMC, that the payment of the principal and interest of this Note is expressly subordinated in right of payment to the payment in full of up to $3.0 million in principal and interest of Senior Indebtedness of the Company. Upon any terminating liquidation of assets of the Company, upon the occurrence of any dissolution; winding up; liquidation, whether or not in bankruptcy; insolvency; or receivership proceedings, the Company shall not pay thereafter, and the Holder of this Note shall not be entitled to receive thereafter, any amount in respect of the principal and interest of this Note unless and until the above specified amount of Senior Indebtedness shall have been paid or otherwise discharged.

The Holder hereof, by its acceptance of this Note, covenants and agrees for itself, its successors, and assigns that in the event of the Company's default hereunder and if the Holder obtains judgment thereon in a court of competent jurisdiction, the Holder shall not execute such judgment upon the assets of the Company, its successors, and assigns unless and until, and only to the extent that, the then book value of such assets exceeds the total amount of Senior Indebtedness, not to exceed $3.0 million.

This Note may be prepaid at any time without penalty.

The Company hereby waives presentment for payment, protest, notice of protest, notice of nonpayment, and diligence in bringing

Page 3

suit. The Company agrees to pay all costs of collection, including reasonable attorney's fees, if a default shall occur under this Note.

The Holder, upon acceptance hereof, shall have no further claims against the Company or any surviving or successor entity, should the Company be sold or acquired, or against the Company's subsidiaries or against their employees for payment and specifically no claims against the subsidiaries (or their assets) of the Company presently owned, or hereafter acquired, except as set forth herein. The Holder specifically releases the Company and its subsidiaries from any further claim except the amount specified by this Note.

IN WITNESS WHEREOF, the undersigned has executed and delivered this Note the day and year written below.

ACCEPTED AND AGREED TO:

By: _____ Date: _____
      Your Name, Chairman
      Survival Management
      Corporation

By: _____ Date: _____
      Holder's Name

Title: _____
      Holder's Title

Company Name: _____

Essential Books for Your Business Book Shelf
(To order, please use the form on the last page)

The Complete Franchise Book by Dennis L. Foster $17.95

What you must know, and are rarely told, about buying or starting your own franchise. A classic by one of the nation's foremost experts on franchising.

Importing Into the United States and *Exporting From the United States* by the U.S. Department of Commerce and the U.S. Customs Service $17.95

Two official publications that offer clear, step-by-step guidance to the fine points of overseas transactions.

How to Become a Successful Consultant in Your Own Field by Hubert Bermont $19.95

This Fortune Book Club selection will show you how to make between $60 to $1000 an hour using the knowledge you already have.

TV/PR by Chambers and Asher $24.95

Learn how to promote yourself, your product, or service on television without having to pay for advertising. Free publicity has catapulted more than one business to national prominence.

How to Build a Million Dollar Fortune by Tyler G. Hicks $17.95

A no-nonsense guide to taking the dream of wealth and turning it into living-color reality.

Mail Order Secrets by Tyler G. Hicks $19.95

Mail order is a low-cost, high-potential way of marketing. New entrepreneurs as well as heads of companies that haven't taken full advantage of this distribution system cannot skip this mentoring manual.

Breakthrough Thinking by Gerald Nadler, Ph.D. and Shozo Hibino $19.95

This international collaboration will teach you a revolutionary way to solve problems, as practiced by the most innovative companies in the world.

FILL IN AND MAIL...TODAY

PRIMA PUBLISHING
P.O. Box 1260ADS
Rocklin, CA 95677

USE YOUR VISA/MC AND ORDER BY PHONE
(916) 624-5718 (M–F 9–4 PST)

Dear People at Prima,
I'd like to order copies of the following titles:

Quantity	Title	Amount
_____	_____	_____
_____	_____	_____
_____	_____	_____
_____	_____	_____
_____	_____	_____

Subtotal $_____

Postage & Handling $___3.00___

Sales Tax $_____

TOTAL (U.S. funds only) $_____

☐ Check enclosed for $ _____ (payable to Prima Publishing)

Charge my   ☐ MasterCard   ☐ VISA

Account No. _____ Exp. Date _____

Signature _____

Your Name _____

Address _____

City/State/Zip _____

Daytime Telephone _____

YOU MUST BE SATISFIED, OR YOUR MONEY BACK!!!
Thank You for Your Order